ELECTING A PRESIDENT

ELECTING A PRESIDENT

by *DUANE BRADLEY*

Decorations by Henry R. Martin

D. VAN NOSTRAND COMPANY, INC.
PRINCETON, NEW JERSEY   *toronto · new york · london*

D. VAN NOSTRAND COMPANY, INC.
120 Alexander St., Princeton, New Jersey (*Principal office*)
24 West 40 Street, New York 18, New York

D. Van Nostrand Company, Ltd.
358, Kensington High Street, London, W.14, England

D. Van Nostrand Company (Canada), Ltd.
25 Hollinger Road, Toronto 16, Canada

Published simultaneously in Canada by
D. Van Nostrand Company (Canada), Ltd.

Library of Congress Catalog Card No. 63–20489

CONTENTS

We do not say
that a man who takes no
interest in politics
minds his own business.

We say
he has no business here at all.

PERICLES

Chapter 1

THE IMPORTANCE
OF THE PRESIDENT

Every four years in America the very air around us begins to crackle with excitement. Billboards, badges, balloons, radios, televisions, newspapers, posters, and even potholders and paper matches scream that we must vote for one candidate or another for President of the United States.

Our President has been called the most important man in the world, because he is the leader of those who stand for freedom. Since it is the voters who elect him, they must be even more important than he.

The idea of a President as the leader of a nation originated in our country. Most of the rest of the world, and many in America, thought it was a very poor idea.

History seemed to prove that people had to be governed with a firm hand, or they were always causing trouble. A firm hand meant a ruler with absolute power. If people were to be allowed to select a leader for themselves, how could he persuade or force them to obey him?

The Americans who thought up this peculiar idea had already proved themselves unruly, disobedient, and rebellious. In each of the three different types of colonies set up in this country there had been attempts to coerce the government. Finally the colonies had banded together and begun a war against the supreme government of the land, the English crown. When this war was won, and each of the separate thirteen newly formed states set up its own government, there were even rebellions against some of them. It seemed obvious to many observers that what the Americans needed was not the right to choose any ruler they wished (whom they could also impeach), but a very strong government which was too strong to be disobeyed.

There had been a great deal of talk about freedom before and during the Revolution, but what did it mean? There was no real proof that ordinary men knew what to do with freedom, and even Samuel Adams, who had helped foment the Revolution, took a dim view of it. "So great is the wickedness of some men, and the stupid servility of others, that one would be almost inclined to conclude that communities cannot be free," he said.

We sometimes think that our government, and the ideas behind it, came into being automatically and completely with the winning of the Revolution against England. This is not true. Our first President was elected in 1789, but the Constitution did not provide for all of the people to have a voice in choosing him. Each state was allowed to select a certain number of electors, and these electors, in turn, selected the President. It was supposed that the electors would be men of knowledge and wide experience and obviously more suited to the task than the average person.

Since then our way of electing a President has changed, and each change has been toward giving more power to the individual voter. In our 200 years of history we have gone further and further down a path that seemed most dangerous when our Constitution was written. Now electors are voted for by the people, and they are not chosen for themselves, but for the candidate whom they represent.

They are not required by law to vote for that candidate, but, as President Woodrow Wilson said, an elector is now a sort of bellpunch to the hand of his party convention. It gives the pressure, and he rings. The party convention selects the candidate, the elector is pledged to support the candidate, and the voter thinks of the candidate when he marks his ballot.

When we go into the voting booth, we look at the name of the presidential candidate and not of the elector, certain that he will vote as pledged. We thus elect our own President, and many of us could not tell the name of the elector for whom we have actually voted.

How powerful is the President whom we elect? He is the head of a government with vast financial resources and the leader of our armed services who number in the millions. Many kings in the past, in far smaller countries, have had the power of life and death over their subjects. Our President is as bound by our laws as we are. He can do only what the Constitution allows and can raise his hand against no man except as the law upholds him.

The powers given to the President by our Constitution have increased with the passing years. This is partly because each President has seen his office and duties differently, and partly because conditions in our country have changed.

Because our relations with the rest of the world have changed, the role of the President has changed in another way.

He is the voice, in world discussions, of almost 200,000,000 people who elected him freely because he represents the things they believe are important.

In the years since George Washington was our first President, we have had many others; some weak, some strong, some outstanding, and a few who made little impression on history. We seem to elect, each time, a man who represents the sum total of our thoughts on government at the moment—and sometimes we have been more interested in our government than at others.

A few Presidents have seemed rather unpromising when elected and have turned into brilliant and courageous leaders. Some who seemed well fitted for the presidency apparently accomplished little.

Whatever his characteristics, though, the man who is our President immediately becomes an international figure. His decisions are studied eagerly, his opinions on international affairs are a matter of grave concern, and even his personal life becomes fascinating to others. A President wields so much power it is safe to say that he can lead us into war or away from it, or change the economic structure of our country. Both have been done by Presidents in our past. Therefore, while the president is bound by our laws and is a servant to our Constitution, it would be difficult to say where his vast power ends. When we make our selection in the voting booth, we take a grave responsibility in our hands.

Just as Samuel Adams said, there are many who are

willing to obey when others speak and so do not think for themselves. There are people who are mentally lazy, who are not really interested in our government, and who never try to understand the issues involved. More than this, there are hundreds of thousands of people who never make use of their votes. Under our system, the vote of each man counts the same, no matter who the man may be or why he votes as he does.

Our founding fathers knew the weaknesses of human nature and wondered if people at large could be trusted to govern themselves. If you have listened to people discussing politics, you may wonder how we ever agree on one man for President when there are so many different opinions.

If you listen to candidates for office and read their campaign material, you may wonder how any voter can make an intelligent decision. Each candidate thinks he is best for the job and that his opponent will bring disaster to the country. Each of our two major political parties believes that it alone has the recipe for our future welfare, and that the other is wrong.

(The ancient Greeks, who also held elections, refused to let a candidate campaign for office. They thought it was unfair. One candidate might be handsomer than another, or a better speaker, but not turn out to be so good at the job for which he was elected).

How do we select a President? How many people

should be allowed to vote for him? Is our President always the choice of the majority of the voters? What about those who vote against the successful candidate? Do they have a right to be represented in our government?

These questions concern us today, and they concerned our forefathers even more—they, after all, were embarking on a new venture with very little to guide them. Their way of electing a President was not exactly ours, and they did not let as large a percentage of people vote, as we do. They gave a better representation to those who voted for the losing candidate, since the one with the second largest number of votes became Vice-President. If this happened today, it would mean that the President would be of one political party and the Vice-President of another, which would be a strange situation.

During World War II, Americans heard a great deal about the Four Freedoms—freedom of speech, freedom to worship, freedom from want, and freedom from fear. These phrases were given to us by President Franklin D. Roosevelt, and once they were ours they became a part of our life. It was something we had known before, but suddenly it became much more clear.

Each of us wants to be able to say what he believes to be true, to worship in his own way, to know that his country will not let him starve, and that he will not be terrorized by private individuals or government agents. Life in a democracy has taught us that if we want these things for ourselves, we must guarantee them to others.

This is the purpose of our government—to keep us as free as possible while giving us the most security possible. What would happen to our government if we lost the right to elect the President of our choice? Would we lose all of our other freedoms at the same time?

It is possible that we would. Let us use our imaginations and see how it might come about. We go to the polls every four years to vote for the candidate of our choice. Before he became a candidate, he had to win many other battles. He had to begin as an ordinary citizen and become prominent enough to attract the attention of his party. He then had to prove to his party that he, and he alone, could win enough votes to make the party victorious in the coming election.

While he is in office, he knows that he is being watched by his party members, by all of those who voted for him, and by everyone who has an interest in how our country is being run. He must answer to these people for everything that he does and says. He owes a debt to everyone who helped put him in office, and he must prove to his opponents that his policies and those of his party are good for the country. (We should remember that Republican candidates are sometimes voted for by Democrats, and Democratic candidates by Republicans. There is also a large group of voters who may go either way in any election, or affect the results just as much by staying at home and not voting at all.)

A President who went further than merely displeasing his party or his opponents, and seemed to place the country in danger, might be impeached. Therefore, a President who is elected freely is answerable to all of us.

Suppose, though, that by some means a President took office and knew he could not be dislodged. The amount of power this would give him can hardly be calculated. He would no longer need to consider what anyone thought, but could do as he pleased. No legislators or lower officials could successfully oppose him, and the voice of public opinion about his actions would be helpless.

America has sometimes been criticized because its government is so fluid. Foreign powers have said that it seems useless to reach an agreement with one administration, knowing that another with a different viewpoint may come into power in a few years. There is some truth in this, but there is more truth in the fact that the very changes in our government preserve our freedoms. There is a saying in New England, "If you don't like the weather, wait five minutes and it will change." We can say of our government, "If you don't like it, wait four years and you can change it."

Before very long, you will be a voter. As you inherit the world from those who have gone before, you will also inherit the right to mark your secret ballot in the privacy of a voting booth. No one has a way of knowing how you mark your own ballot, but the world soon sees the result of the way you voted.

It may be your great privilege to elect to office a President of the United States who will help to spread freedom throughout the world and bring peace and safety to all countries.

Whether this happens or not will depend on you. In the course of our history since the Constitution was adopted, the changes that have taken place have given more and more power to the individual American voter until he may well be called the most important man in the world.

Chapter 2

CORNING AND BEANING IN THE COLONIES

If our early American ancestors had been different, we might not now have the right to vote for our own President.

The colonies in America were a part of the British Empire, and Americans thought of themselves as having the same rights as any other English citizens. The trouble began when a few men began to tell them that they had other rights, too, simply because they were human beings. These rights were not granted by the English crown, nor were they widely recognized as being due to the average man.

Why did these ideas about freedom and equal justice and government by the consent of the governed gain such ground in this new country? Perhaps it was something about the air in America, or maybe it was because the English government let their colonies in the new land run on a free rein for a number of years. At any rate, the colonists soon began to make demands that the English crown found difficult to understand.

These demands were the cornerstone of our first Constitution, so it is interesting to see how they came about.

When the first settlers came to our shores and set up communities, the need for a local government was almost as important as the need for food and shelter. Each man had to depend on himself for some things, but for others he had to depend on the group.

He could cut down trees by himself, plant his own grain, and care for his own milk cow, but he had to agree with others about property boundaries and joining together for mutual aid and defense. Anyone who has ever been a member of a club, or tried to work with any group to get them to accomplish some project together, can understand how necessary it was to create some central authority in each little community.

It is very probable that these early governments were somewhat informal and that every able-bodied, or contributing, male member of the community had his say in what was done. To a group of settlers trying to carve a home out of the wilderness, government was a matter of life and death. They did not meet together to decide trivial matters but to agree on how they might survive. In the homeland, government might well have been left to established officials, but in our own early communities those who were affected by the government had a voice in it.

This statement does not apply to parish, county, or colony government. Officials on that level were elected on a different basis, and each colony might have its own regulations on this score.

There were three kinds of colonies in America, with three different kinds of government—the chartered, the royal, and the proprietary. In some respects, they had a great deal in common.

Massachusetts Bay Colony was a *chartered* colony, operating under a charter granted to a joint-stock company. Under this charter, a General Court of the freemen met four times a year to elect a governor and eighteen assistants and to make laws not contrary to those of England. The word "freemen" gives us a clue as to how this colony was actually run.

Not every settler in Massachusetts Bay Colony was a "freeman," and only freemen could vote in colony elections.

Each colony had its own requirements for "freemen," but they were generally about the same. Often he had to be a member of the Church in good standing (Church and State were not separate yet in this country), had to own a certain amount of property or money, and perhaps be the head of a household. In some cases he had to be a resident in the area from which he voted; in others he merely had to own property there. In some colonies a freeman had to be of good character, and could prove this by a voucher signed by the local minister. (If it later proved untrue that his character was good, some colonies provided that the minister signing the voucher could be fined five pounds.)

There is strong sentiment in this country now against any such restrictions on voting, but it is easy to see why our forefathers required them. While the settlers had come to this country in many cases to escape the lack of freedom of expression in the Old World, they were not always willing to grant this same freedom to those who did not agree with them.

We would be aghast today if anyone suggested that only members of a certain church could vote, or even those who belonged to any church. This was far from true in the early colonies. The Church (and there was only one in many colonies) was a part of the government. When each town built a "meeting-house," it was used for both church services and town government meetings. People who braved the dangers of creating a new life in a strange country in order to be free to worship God did not intend to hazard their project by letting those who did not agree with them rule their lives.

The tendency today is toward the belief that it is not only safe but necessary for every adult to be allowed to vote if our democracy is to be preserved. Our ancestors had neither our faith in democracy nor our understanding of it.

They had come from countries in which different classes of people were quite distinct, and in which the right to rule was believed to come from God. "The divine right of kings" was taken for granted, and most people believed that some men were born to govern just as others were born to till the soil.

Such a belief was hard to lose immediately. If you had been poor and hungry most of your life and saw a few very wealthy, beautifully dressed, and magnificent people from time to time, it would be easy to believe that these people were as different from you as they appeared to be.

We can understand this better if we think of an average group of students in a high school today. Some of them will be good athletes, and others will be good students. Some will be more attractive than others, and some will have special skills. We recognize these qualities and see nothing wrong in accepting these basic differences in people. Our ancestors saw the right and the ability to govern in the same light—as a natural law of nature.

In the early New England colonies, most people believed in predestination. This meant that the whole world and the fate of man were planned in advance by God, and man could do nothing about it. If God favored a certain man, He showed this favor by blessing him with worldly power and influence. Obviously, if God thought certain people were better than others, and showed it through their prosperity, who was the average man to question His will?

A new influence must have begun working to start the yeast of equal rights fermenting. Once people were faced with the rigors of a fight for survival, it became apparent that certain characteristics were even more important than wealth and position. A man of wealth and property might not be very useful in waging war against the Indians, while a man of low birth might prove himself a real leader. More than this, the settlers were without some of the natural protection from the elements that the civilization of Europe had provided them.

The instinct to be independent was rooted in the circumstances of their lives. A settler who moved into the wilderness, cut down trees to make a field, built his own house and defended it, soon began to get the idea that he did almost everything for himself. There were no policemen or soldiers to depend on, and few assets except those he provided. Like a youngster who goes away from home and begins to earn his own living, the American colonist began to be reluctant to take orders from his parent country.

He also began to disagree with the government in his own colony when he felt it was unfair.

In 1631, in Massachusetts Bay Colony, a protest was made against taxation without representation. Two years later fourteen towns sent representatives to Boston to demand a view of the original charter, which they believed was being violated by the government.

Virginia became a *royal province* in 1652. A House of Burgesses was a representative group composed of two representatives from each local unit of the colony. The rest of the government was made up of a governor and six councilors, appointed by the king. The governor and the six councilors acted as the executive, the high court of justice, and the upper house of the legislature. Like the General Court of the Massachusetts Bay Colony, this assembly could make laws which were not contrary to the laws of England. In 1676 the people became so disturbed because of economic distress, high taxes, and the failure of the governor to wage war against the Indians, that they rose in rebellion under Nathaniel Bacon. This forced the governor to dissolve the assembly, and a new one was appointed which passed a series of laws to provide more democracy.

Pennsylvania was a *proprietary* colony, with William Penn as founder, and had almost complete home rule. The Penn family appointed the governors, but the people were allowed to elect both houses of government and to be as free as possible. Conflict arose in this colony because the longer settled and more wealthy eastern counties had the major share of representation—the three counties of Chester, Bucks, and Philadelphia elected twenty-six delegates, while the five frontier counties elected only ten.

It seems clear then that, while our forefathers were not given as much influence over their immediate government as we, they found ways to make their opinions felt. Even those without the vote learned to influence others, and almost from the beginning there were rebellions against any government which the people felt failed to protect them or restricted their activities.

Rebellions against government were no new thing in Europe, but many of these rebellions were led by powerful men trying to increase their power. They were rebellions against other men, and not necessarily rebellions against certain principles. In America, struggles with the government tended to be people fighting for more rights for themselves and what was being called "freedom."

Because of all of these things, the average man in early America was as interested in all phases of government as his descendant is apt to be in the World Series. Men met in taverns and on the village green to talk about laws and how they were made, governments and how they operated. Government in this new country was not some far off and lofty thing symbolized by rich robes and gleaming crowns—it was a vital element in everyday life. If a town voted to raise taxes, the average man had to pay them, and he had learned to argue about it at town meeting. If his representative to the general assembly voted for more protection against the Indians, and the general assembly failed to concur, it was his life that might be lost.

We sometimes forget that our history does not begin with the Declaration of Independence, but early in the 1600s. In the period from 1600 to 1775, America was like a gigantic political laboratory, with one experiment after another being tried to see which was best for governing men.

Many of the settlers could neither read nor write. How, then, could they vote? The solution was to use what was at hand, and so the system of "corning and beaning" came about.

In several colonies, beans or grains of corn were used for votes. Sometimes both beans and corn were used, a bean being a vote in the negative and a grain of corn a vote in the affirmative. When either corn or beans alone were used, a white one meant yes, a black one meant no.

The beans or corn were placed in a receptacle near where those in charge of the election presided, and names were probably checked off the list of legal voters to be sure no fraud was committed. When the election was closed, the receptacles were opened, the contents counted and the results could then be declared.

An illiterate American settler, living in a log cabin and voting by dropping a grain of corn in a container, does not seem much like our picture of a great political philosopher. And yet it was from just such men that our democracy came.

Chapter 3

A TOWN IS BORN

America has always been a refuge for those who have suffered from tyranny and oppression in their homelands. Some of these refugees have found America hard to understand.

A Jewish rabbi, who escaped from his native Hungary with his wife and child during World War II, sat down with a writer several years later and explained what it was like.

"When I was born in Hungary," he said, "we had our own government and did not consider that we were unfortunate. Later the Germans conquered us and we lived under a dictatorship, and then we were occupied by Russia. We suffered a great deal under these two different occupation governments, but I think they would not have been possible except for the way we had lived before.

"My son, who was born in a prison camp, is now twelve years old. Today his civics class visited our state capital and, although I have now lived here several years and read all that I can find about our government, I could hardly believe what he told me.

"The state legislature was in session—busy, important men working hard to govern the state. When my son's class went to the capital, the legislature halted its business so that they could be introduced. They were welcomed by the governor himself, who said that it was wonderful for young people to visit the capital and learn how the state is run, because sometime they will be in charge of it themselves."

The rabbi paused to laugh.

"I must tell you that, as a European, I sometimes feel that young people in this country have too many liberties and too much freedom, but this made me think.

"When I was a child growing up, I never said to my father, 'No, I do not want to do that,' or asked him 'Why?' when he gave me an order. In our family, as in other families, the father was the ruler. When he spoke, everyone obeyed. As an American father, I speak—and my children sit down and discuss it with me.

"I went to school at the age of five, and in the school the teacher was the absolute ruler. We had no student government, and no informal question-and-answer sessions in our classrooms. The teacher told us what to do and what to learn, and we obeyed him.

"When we walked on the streets, we saw policemen. If they said we were disobeying a law, we knew that they were right. In this country I have seen people get a traffic ticket for overparking, and tell the policeman that the meter did not work, or that some mistake had been made, and the policeman listened to them. In our country, that did not happen.

"It was the same in every phase of our life. Each of us had his place and stayed in it. We accepted the idea that certain people had charge of different areas of our lives, and we never questioned them or argued with them. When our country was defeated and we had to obey different governments, they were more rigid and harsh, but we had been trained from birth to stay in our place and to do what we were told."

The rabbi lives in our time, but he has much in common with the people who came to America to settle the new country. For centuries everything was more or less settled into a pattern and only the very daring or the most discontented worked to change it.

Why did those who settled on our shores eventually demand and create a government such as they had never seen, and which was actually a quite dangerous experiment? The early Americans were in much the same position as will be the first settlers on another planet, and yet, in a way, they had even less to guide them.

In Europe their ancestors had usually stayed throughout their lives in one town, with settled laws and customs which molded their lives. If they moved to another town, they found it equally well established and had very little opportunity to change what they did not like.

When they came to America, they did not find, but created, towns—and a town is much more than a group of houses and farms. It is a number of people living closely together and agreeing among themselves as to how their lives will be regulated.

Before the passengers on the *Mayflower* disembarked, they held a meeting which has been called "the first town meeting of New England." They drew up a covenant which listed the laws they agreed among themselves to observe. Each town created afterward followed this pattern, and although most of them were similar, each one was an example of men doing and learning something new and strange.

Perhaps we can understand better by following the creation of one particular town from the beginning.

In 1690, some men from Middlesex and Worcester counties of Massachusetts went with an expedition against Canada to avenge unprovoked atrocities committed by Indians and their French allies against

American frontier towns. The expedition went by sea to Quebec, but found the town so heavily fortified that an attack would have been useless, so it returned to Boston.

The men who took part in the expedition were paid in paper money (the first ever seen in New England), which soon became so depreciated that it was almost worthless.

Forty years later those of the group who were still living petitioned the General Court of Massachusetts for grants of land as compensation for their services. The settled towns were becoming crowded, and venturous souls wanted to move farther out into the wilderness and set up new homes for themselves. Eight townships in Massachusetts were granted in response to this petition.

In 1728 John Whitman, Esq. petitioned the General Court for a grant of land six miles square, and not until 1735 were he and the group he headed given the right to a township of that size on a line between the Merrimac and Connecticut rivers. In September 1737, Mr. Whitman met in Concord, Massachusetts, with sixty grantees to make plans for the new township, which was called Number 6.

We might say that this meeting, held almost half a century after the expedition for which the township was payment, was the first official town meeting of what later became Henniker, New Hampshire. In a way it was a beginning, but everything that happens has roots deep in the past.

These men had assumed the responsibility of creating a new town almost entirely on their own. In order to do that they had to sit down together and work out ways of proceeding. This meeting almost certainly followed a pattern of procedure and behavior that had begun long ago.

The man in charge of this early town meeting was called the moderator, just as he is today. Another man, called a clerk, kept a record of everything that happened. The people present were those legally entitled to have a voice in the matter, or the voters—in this case, the proprietors of Number 6. The clerk had a list of their names to identify them and assure their right to be heard.

Very probably the moderator, who called the meeting to order and conducted it, held a gavel in his hand. In Europe he might have worn some special garment or badge of office which represented his authority. In this country he usually did not.

The gavel, which is used so widely in almost every sort of official meeting, has a long ancestry. The Teutonic tribes of Europe held meetings to decide what they would do, and their leader held a "talking stick" as emblem of his authority. When another man wanted a chance to talk, he was given the talking stick and could hold the floor until the leader directed him to pass it on to someone else who could then speak.

If John Whitman, Esq. and the other proprietors of Number 6 thought they were well on the way to having a town of their own when they held their meeting in Concord, Massachusetts, they were sadly mistaken.

The colony of New Hampshire did not want Massachusetts establishing towns within what she felt were her boundaries, and so trouble arose. It could not be settled without an appeal to the crown. Both Massachusetts and New Hampshire sent agents to present their claims to the king of England. The king's decision was that the township of Number 6 lay in New Hampshire and not Massachusetts, so the original proprietors lost all claim to it.

In 1774 some of the original proprietors petitioned the General Court of Massachusetts for a different township in Massachusetts to repay them for all of the trouble and expense they had been to on behalf of Number 6. The petition said they had spent money to build roads and mills, which was not exactly true. Money had been spent for a mill, but those who came to establish it were frightened by Indians and left before they had accomplished much.

Some faint marks had been made, though, in that part of the wilderness which was called Number 6.

In 1748 a new group of men met in Londonderry,

New Hampshire, for the purpose of trying to obtain a New Hampshire township. At this meeting a treasurer was chosen, since money was involved and some one had to be responsible for it. A committee was appointed to get an accounting from the treasurer as to the amount of money he had and what he had done with it. (Democracy works best when it has a system of checks and balances, with no single person given complete authority to act unquestioned by anyone else.) Another committee was appointed to petition the New Hampshire government for land for a township.

Four years later another meeting was held to further the business and it was decided to take in eighty, ninety, or a hundred proprietors for the new township, if they could be found.

Perhaps some of those who had originally been interested had lost faith in the venture, because the report of this meeting has a rather sad note at the end. It was decided that, after the petition for a township had been made, notice would be given at the two meetinghouses in Londonderry for two successive Sabbath days of a meeting where the petitioners would give their report. The record ends, "And then the Committee shall Call the petitioners together to hear there Report and the Petitioners that Doth not appear will be Lookt upon as Dropping the whole affair."

Chapter 4

THE ROOTS OF DEMOCRACY

In May another meeting was held, at which it was decided that every petitioner had to pay more money, and if he did not he would lose his status. If he dropped out immediately he could have his original investment returned. A group was selected to look over two different plots of land that might be available as townsites and to report on them.

In July of that year the petitioners were given a grant for their long-awaited township. There were now fifty-nine of them, each named in the grant, and they agreed to support a minister of the gospel, to build a meetinghouse, and to set aside land with a suitable stream for the establishment of a mill, to reserve all suitable white pine for masts for His Majesty's Navy, and to divide the land on a fair basis.

The new township, which began to seem a reality,

was still known as Number 6, since that was the plot decided upon and it still held the original name. The land was surveyed and the property of each proprietor allocated; a committee was appointed to see about getting a mill established, and a practice that is still followed in New Hampshire towns was voted. In the original spelling of the record of the meeting, it was voted to "chews a Com-tee to Pramblat the Town Lins and Renew their Reang Staks." If this seems like a foreign language, we must remember that spelling was not regulated as it is now, and each particular writer spelled the words as they sounded to him.

In this case, the vote was to choose a committee to perambulate the town lines and renew the range stakes.

The original township was laid out in a rectangle with a large tree marking each of the four corners. Ranges, or strips of land to be later made into roads, were left between each two lots, and these were marked with oak stakes surrounded by a pile of rocks. It was important to check these from time to time because the township of Number 6 was still nothing more than a plot of land in the middle of the wilderness, inhabited only by Indians, animals, and birds, completely isolated and unguarded. In time to come, the land might have great value, but at this point anyone could have changed range stakes to suit himself unless they were checked regularly.

As time passed, more meetings were held and more decisions were made. Proof of this is the article in the warrant for a meeting to be held in 1757: "To see if the proprietors will chews a Commite to Perambulate their lind betwixt Hopkinton and No Six and Renew the Reang Lind there In order to Prevent troball that may otherwise hapan their Neglecting the same."

Even as today, town meetings (though the town did not yet exist) had warrants. A warrant is an announcement of the meeting, with a list of items (called articles) to be discussed and decided. Today any article may be put on a warrant if enough people sign a petition to have it included. In those times, a similar practice was probably followed.

We must remember that the meeting in Londonderry in November of 1748 to try to find land for a town was now nine years in the past. Since then many of the Londonderry proprietors had dropped out and new ones had been added, the town itself had been surveyed and laid out, a charter had been granted, but there was still no town. Hope must have faltered again.

The next year, in March, a committee was appointed to perambulate the line between Number 6 and Hopkinton, and two years later another committee was appointed to do the same thing. It seems that the first committee had never acted.

In 1762 a few of the braver souls decided that something definite must be done about Number 6. A meeting was called, to be held in the home of one of the proprietors in Londonderry: officers were elected, and some business was conducted. It was voted that "a path a horse could tread on" was to be cleared from the east end of Number 6 to the center of the town, and that two men were to be paid for doing the work.

Another year went by and another meeting was held, but nothing much was accomplished. In the meantime, though, people had begun moving into Number 6 . . . only a few families, but the wilderness had begun to be a home to American settlers. There was need now for highways and the preaching of the gospel.

In 1766 this business was transacted at a meeting. The owner of each right in Number 6 was to pay a half dollar to hire a preacher of the gospel and two shillings to pay for clearing and repairing the highways. At another meeting later in the same year it was voted to change the highways where the land was not suitable for them, to clear three acres in the center lot for a burial ground and a meetinghouse, and to raise five shillings on each right to defray town expenses.

In 1768 the township of Number 6 was finally in-corporated and the town of Henniker was born.

It had been a long and stormy journey, but men had met together, discussed, voted on what action to take, and "borned" a town.

In creating a town, they had created a way of life.

When they gained rights to a plot of land, it was only the beginning of starting a town. The crown of England, and the royal governor of New Hampshire, could give them the right to land, could demand that they "maintain good order and encourage the culture of the land" and save the best white pine for masts for the king's Navy, but all of the rest was up to the settlers themselves.

It is a hazardous, difficult, and lonely job to walk into a strange forest and clear space for a cabin. It takes strength and endurance to cut huge trees, shape them into logs for a cabin, open a clearing for a garden, break the virgin earth and plant it with seeds. It takes courage to shelter a family against weather and misfortune, against the dangers of starva-tion and Indians. All of these things, though, are simple, direct, and plain.

The greatest job done by our forefathers was learn-ing to govern themselves. It is far from easy to work with a group of men, many of whom are of different backgrounds and different opinions, and learn how to cooperate to get a job finished.

The men who created Henniker had first to learn to meet together and reach decisions; then they had to learn to deal with those in authority who could grant them their wishes. They had to raise money, on a fair basis, and arrange for it to be spent wisely in their best interests. They had to understand all of the problems involved in surveying a township, dividing land, marking boundaries and maintaining them, and getting along well with neighboring villages. They had to meet disappointments in dealing with both disinterested authority and the fainthearted among themselves. They had to meet the conditions set by the government granting them the land and to deal with many who knew more than they about laws and politics, and yet maintain their own rights.

Very shortly after the incorporation of Henniker, the town held a meeting to handle immediate problems, but the first official town meeting was held March 6, 1769, in the home of Silas Barnes. Highways and town offices were discussed and money raised for town expenses. The matter of a school house came up, and a motion carried to raise twenty dollars for it, but only ten dollars for other town expenses.

The names of some of the officers elected in early times are almost as strange to us as if they referred to a foreign country. In New England, for example, the town meeting elected a town clerk, a town constable, three selectmen, surveyors of highways and surveyors of fences (to be sure no one encroached on his neighbor's property), tithing men, sealers of leather, sealers of weights and measures, hog reeves, and field drivers. They hired the minister and saw that he was paid, they arranged to have the meeting-house built, and they made pounds in which to keep stray animals. They voted on how to defend themselves from Indians (some of the towns complained bitterly that they were given neither money nor help for this purpose from the state government and had to do it all themselves), and they often disagreed violently about every issue that arose.

If the temper of the town was bad, because of severe weather, poor harvests, or excessive trouble with one thing or another, they might sit down and vote to do absolutely nothing. On an article in one town meeting to see how much money the town would raise to pay the selectmen for their services for the last few years, they voted to pay them nothing. At the same meeting they voted not to raise any money for schools, and the next year they voted to let the hogs run wild through the town.

The muscles of democracy were flexed in these early town meetings, just as they are today. It gave a man a sense of power to think of an article for the town warrant, to find enough signers for it, to make the motion that would bring it to a vote in meeting, and to see it succeed.

On issues of colony-wide importance, meetings were held in the capital, and representatives were sent from towns. On issues requiring the vote of all freemen, something else had to be concocted. There was so much work to be done in the new communities that not all men entitled to a vote could afford to leave home and be gone for the length of time it would take to attend such a meeting. Few of them, however, wanted to lose the chance to express an opinion. The solution was interesting.

Votes on issues which would be taken up at larger meetings were made in the same way as those for the local meeting. If corn and beans were used, these were put into special containers, and the containers sealed. They were carried to the place of the larger meeting and opened when the other votes were to be counted. It was years before it occurred to someone that there was a considerable waste of time and effort involved in this procedure. After that, the votes were counted at the local meeting, the results tabulated, and the final score taken to the larger meeting.

By the time the Revolution began, Americans knew a great deal about government. Were they frightened and uneasy at the thought of being cut off from their mother country? Until that time, the

English government had been behind them, solid and secure. Most of them prided themselves on being Englishmen, with all of the prestige that word denoted. How did it feel to them to know suddenly that their own small hand-hewn governments, with none of the tradition and stability of the long-established crown of England, were all they had for defense?

The answer may be found in the minutes of town meetings held during that period. There is only one difference to be detected. In addition to selecting officers and raising money for highways, schools, and meetinghouses, there were new problems. Representatives were elected to meet with the Provincial Congress to help decide how to restore and improve the rights of the colonies; money was raised to pay the men who had gone to fight the British in the first battles, and ways were contrived to raise the allotted troops from each town, outfit and provide for them till "all are maid equal with each other in services."

Americans did not seem especially disturbed at the thought of being on their own—in their own minds they had been on their own all the time.

Chapter 5

HIS HIGHNESS, THE PRESIDENT

The war we fought against England for our independence was a long and hard one. When it was finally over and the soldiers could return to their families and their homes, the whole country must have breathed a sigh of relief.

At last liberty belonged to America. Now men were free and could build a country to fit their dreams, unhindered by despotism.

It would be hard to say just how long this pleasant illusion lasted, or how soon men began to realize that liberty is not won forever by a war, nor a perfect government created from hope.

In Massachusetts, as in some of the other states, things began to go wrong. During the Revolution, Massachusetts had been governed under a constitution only slightly different from the royal charter, and in

1780 it had written a new one. (Other colonies had written new constitutions earlier, but the Bay State wanted to wait until it was sure it would make no mistakes.) This constitution provided that it could not be amended for fifteen years; it required that voters be property owners and that officeholders own property in scale with the office they held.

Massachusetts also had debtors' prisons, and this was one of the things that led to what eventually became a rebellion against the government.

In the western part of the state, times were hard. The war had been costly, and there was no mother country across the seas to pay for it, so everyone felt the pinch. Soldiers had received little pay for their services in the army, homes and farms had suffered from their absence, and the certificates awarded to them by the state for their part in winning the victory were not exchangeable for cash—yet. Most of the veterans had sold their certificates to those who had money, at much less than their face value, in order to raise a little cash.

Money, the kind of hard money that was needed to pay bills and taxes, became so scarce it almost seemed to disappear. Those who could not pay their bills and taxes were called into court. The court often ruled that their property must be sold (for much less than its real value, since no one had enough money to pay good prices), and when the sum realized was not sufficient, men found themselves in debtors' prison. Even worse than this, there were rumors that the government was getting ready to redeem the veterans' certificates at face value. In order to do this, it would probably raise taxes—to be paid by the poverty-stricken farmer already in danger of debtors' prison, and enrich the sharpers who had bought the certificates for so little.

This was certainly not what they had fought for. The government in Boston was as cruel and unreasonable as the one in England they had successfully defied.

When the state legislature went into session, the poorer counties, who suffered most, often could not afford to send their legal representatives to attend and plead their cause. Sometimes a county might not even have a citizen wealthy enough to be eligible for the legislature.

Boston, where the legislature met, seemed as remote from the western farmlands as England. There were few newspapers and most people knew only what they heard by word of mouth.

The most obvious thing to be done was exactly what they had done during the war when their freedom had been at stake. County conventions were held to by-pass the regular government, and even the poor farmers could attend them to express their concern about the dreadful state of affairs.

In other states, too, there were rebellions which worried those who were concerned with the welfare of the country. Many people believed that England still hoped to regain control of her former colonies and saw signs of this attempt in things that were happening. Money was scarce in the new country, and too much of it was being spent on luxuries from England—if America went bankrupt, England could easily step in and take over.

Those who had hoped that freedom from England would immediately create a new and glorious way of life in this country found that it was not so easy. America had as many problems as before, and the several rebellions against state governments indicated that it might have even more.

How could these problems be solved? The state governments could call out troops against their own people and enforce their own laws, thus showing they were too strong to be defied. This might prove that the little states, each separate and differently governed than the others, were capable of handling trouble within their own borders. This was one solution.

Some believed that the only governments which could be run fairly were very small town governments. They would have had America composed of hundreds of individual and sovereign towns, loosely related to each other.

Another solution was more radical, and only a

relatively few people believed in it. That was the idea of establishing one central government over the whole country, uniting the states in peace as they had never been truly united during the Revolution.

Under the Articles of Confederation, the states were joined for their mutual defense against a common enemy, but retained their individual sovereignty. The government could ask for support, but could not demand it; it could call for troops and supplies, but not be sure they would appear.

Before the Declaration of Independence, and probably after it, the English government encouraged dissension between the various colonies to try to keep them from joining forces and thus increase their strength.

Although the colonies were known to England as "the United English Colonies of North America," and as "the United States of America" in the Declaration of Independence, they were not truly united except in certain areas.

Some statesmen felt that a single central government would make a stronger country; others felt that this would be too much like being under the rule of England. If the average man had so much trouble with his own state government, what chance would he have with a national government? Trying to cure dissatisfaction with the autocracy of a state government by giving authority to a larger and stronger government seemed a most peculiar solution.

When we look back into the past, many of the things that happened seem reasonable and just, simply because they happened. Today we can hardly conceive of an America in which each separate state is the ruler of its own destiny, but that was what it seemed the people of our country really wanted at that time.

Washington and others who had fought so hard for independence were greatly disturbed by news of the rebellion in Massachusetts and in other states and realized that a drastic step must be taken. Through their efforts, a Constitutional Convention was called, and delegates from the states attended.

The new Constitution, when it was published, was the subject of much heated debate. If it often seems to us that what happens in our capital has little to do with us, it did not seem so to the people of America then. The last few years had taught them that the laws under which they lived were as important as their very lives.

We are often told that it was the rich and powerful men in the young America who shaped our Constitution and that it was designed for the special benefit of just such people. Certainly the Federalists, those who supported it, came mainly from this class.

This makes the Constitution itself, when read carefully, a most peculiar document.

In most of the states, only property owners could vote, and men were not eligible for high office unless they possessed a stated amount of money. How odd, then, to read that even the President of the United States was required only to be a native-born citizen (or a citizen at the time the Constitution was adopted), at least thirty-five years old, and fourteen years a resident of this country. Senators had to be thirty years old, citizens for nine years, and inhabitants of the state which elected them. Representatives had to be twenty-five years of age, citizens for seven years, and inhabitants of the state which elected them. There was no mention of money, title, prestige, property, race, religious affiliation, or even sex—merely simple requirements which thousands then and millions now of our citizens might easily fulfill.

The Constitution could not go into effect until it was ratified by nine of the thirteen colonies, and the battle for this ratification was a bitter one. When the votes were counted, they showed how close the race had been in several colonies. In Massachusetts, the votes were 187 to 168; in New Hampshire fifty-seven to forty-six; in Virginia eighty-nine to seventy-nine, and in New York thirty to twenty-seven. These votes were made by ratifying conventions, which were chosen instead of state legislatures to pass on the Constitution.

As soon as the Constitution was ratified, the first national elections in America were held. Each state was allowed representatives based on total population, and two senators. For the presidential election, each state was required to elect as many electors as it had senators and representatives, who would vote, in their own states, for two persons. The one having the larger portion of votes, if it amounted to a majority, was to be President, and the one with the next largest number would be Vice-President. The votes were to be sent to the seat of the government of the United States, addressed to the president of the Senate, who would then open the votes, count them, and announce the results.

On March 4, 1789, a Wednesday, the first Senate of the United States began its first session in New York City, with eight members present. Since this did not constitute a quorum, they adjourned from day to day until two weeks later, March 18. No more senators had turned up, and so it was decided to send a circular to eight of the nearest members, asking them to attend.

Even so, it was Monday, April 6, before twelve of the newly elected senators had arrived in New York and the official business of the United States of

America could begin. It was first necessary to elect a president of the Senate who could then count the ballots for the President of the United States and declare him elected.

Every elector had voted for George Washington, which gave him sixty-nine votes—the only President in our history to be elected unanimously. John Adams received the next largest total, thirty-four which made him Vice-President.

On Saturday, April 25, a report was received from Charles Thompson, whom the Senate had designated to inform President Washington of his election. Mr. Thompson had a message from the President which said that Mr. Washington would agree to whatever time, place, and manner of inauguration both Houses of the Congress thought proper, but that he did not think the necessary arrangements could be made before the next Thursday.

It was indeed on Thursday, April 30, that the oath of office was administered to President George Washington, in the presence of the assembled members of his new government. After the oath was administered, the Chancellor of the State of New York proclaimed, "Long live George Washington, President of the United States."

Our first President was a man of wealth, prestige, and importance before his election, but the Constitution which created his office also opened it to those without these assets. There can be little doubt, though, that some of our leaders had visions of a presidency that would have the qualities of kingship in other countries, and that they expected a national aristocracy to develop. John Adams, for example, believed that our President should be called "His Highness" or "His Majesty" in order to excite great respect and awe among the people.

On Thursday, May 14, the Senate heard a report from a committee which had been appointed to determine "under what title it will be proper for the Senate to address the President." The committee, having given it careful thought, had what they considered the right answer. The President was to be addressed as "His Highness, the President of the United States of America, and Protector of their Liberties."

It is easy to follow the course of their thoughts. Kings were called "His Highness" and had phrases like "protectors of this and that" after their names. The United States were referred to in the plural, and not in the singular. The new government was, therefore, the head of several separate states, and the President was as close to a king as a title could make him.

Unfortunately for those who had this vision of the proper function of our chief executive and our government, the work of this committee came to nothing.

The Senate had to announce that, though it was convinced the President should have a title of proper dignity and impressiveness, the House of Representatives did not concur. Therefore, in order to preserve harmony between the two bodies, the Senate dropped its own suggestion and agreed that the President should henceforth be addressed as "the President of the United States."

Chapter 6

THE REMARKABLE DOCUMENT

The new government of which George Washington became the first chief executive was, on the surface, little more than a bold experiment. The people in the government did not agree about it, the men who had written the Constitution which created it did not agree about it, and the people who were to be governed by it did not agree about it.

If Americans, as a group, could be said to agree on any one thing, it was that they did not want an American government with the same powers they had resisted on the part of England. When the Constitutional Convention met, many of the liberals who had been prominent in the Revolution were not present. Thomas Jefferson was American minister to Paris, Thomas Paine was also in Europe, Samuel Adams was not elected as a delegate, and Patrick Henry refused to attend because he "smelt a rat" in the proceedings.

Of the sixty-three delegates appointed to the Convention, fifty-five attended. Only thirty-nine of these signed the Constitution, which they had not been elected to write in any case. Their purpose was to rewrite the Articles of Confederation, and instead they had formulated, out of much argument and many differences of opinion, an entirely new document. The most that they could say for it was that, while none of them was entirely satisfied, they felt it was the best they could ever agree upon.

There were many remarkable things about it. One of the most remarkable was the section referring to the election of the President. At a time when even voters had to meet certain requirements before they could vote; when officeholders had to meet even more rigid requirements before they could hold office; when the idea of true democracy was still in an early and formative stage (and considered highly dangerous nonsense by many); the requirements for the highest office in the land were extremely meager.

They are given in Article II, Section 1 of our Constitution: "No Person, except a natural born Citizen, or a Citizen of the United States, at the time of the Adoption of this Constitution, shall be eligible to the Office of President; neither shall any Person be eligible to that Office who shall not have attained to the Age of thirty five Years, and been fourteen Years a Resident within the United States."

Even more than this, the people, however indirectly, were to choose the President themselves by electing the men who would choose him. Under English rule their king had been, so they were told, chosen by God. Now this right was placed within their reach, and as the years have passed it has become wholly theirs.

In order to understand the importance of another part of the procedure of electing a President, we must remember that America was a small country and the number of truly outstanding men in it was quite limited. The general theory of government, at this time, was that only a few able people out of the masses were capable of ruling over others, and one might think that these few had already become known to the country and were holding office. However, Section 1 of Article II of the Constitution said that the men who were actually to elect the President, the electors, were NOT to be senators, representatives, or any persons then holding an office of trust or profit under the United States.

The delegates to the Constitutional Convention might have provided that the regular state officials elect the President, or at least have limited the electors to those of a certain income, race, religion, or social class. Similar restrictions already applied to much lesser offices. Instead they left it up to each state to appoint its own electors, as its own legislature directed.

In Article IV, Section 3, a policy of the Articles of Confederation, which a noted Swiss historian has called "one of the most important laws of the United States, and from the point of world history perhaps the most important," was continued by implied consent. Under this Ordinance, adopted in 1787, a new state could form its own government once it had 60,000 free inhabitants and, on congressional approval, be admitted to the union "on an equal footing with the original states in all respects whatsoever."

Prior to this time, when people from one country settled in another and formed a colony, that colony was considered a possession of the mother country. America was thus a possession of the British Empire, under its jurisdiction and subject to its laws. The Revolution was fought because Americans believed they should not obey a government in which they had no active part.

Too often, in the history of the world, one group of men has fought passionately for certain rights for itself and then just as passionately to keep from extending these rights to others. We can be proud that our ancestors did not do this in respect to any Americans who might go into unsettled areas of the land and set up new states. As new states were formed, they were not to be possessions of the central government, but part of it. Each new state, as it was accepted, was to be equal with all other states, and the votes of its inhabitants would count equally with the votes of the inhabitants of the original states.

The chief officer of the new country was to be selected by the people, as their various state governments decreed. If a state wished, it might have the people vote for the electors, which has eventually become the case in every state. The electors chosen to implement the will of the states were not to be persons already in office, but those outside; new states could be formed, and as they were accepted they became part of, and not a possession of, the government.

It is hard for us to realize how little faith there was in the government which we now know to be the best and strongest on earth. From beginning to end, it was a compromise . . . an attempt to find a few points on which people at large could be brought to agree.

Much of the rest of the world considered it a feeble joke. They did not think that people knew how to govern themselves, or even wished to do so. Some of those who helped create the government were full of doubts and fears. Hamilton called the Constitution a "frail and worthless fabric," and John Adams didn't think the new government would last longer than his own lifetime. It had been difficult to get the support of the nine states required to ratify it, and some still think the majority of the people of America neither approved of the new Constitution nor wanted it. Only about one fourth of the male adults of America were qualified voters, and it has been estimated that about one sixth of them voted to ratify the Constitution.

We should always remember that those who do not vote have an effect on the outcome of any election, though it is often not the effect they wish. Suppose that ten members of a high school class of fifty want to spend class money to buy a trophy. Twenty members may not be interested or think it is important. If the ten eager members can persuade ten more to vote with them, and the twenty disinterested do not attend the meeting, the twenty who vote in the affirmative will win over the ten who do not agree. Twenty is a minority in a group of fifty, but a majority if only thirty vote.

It is possible, then, that apathy as much as eagerness brought our Constitution into being. Those who wanted it fought for it so desperately, and perhaps enough of those who did not care much made so little effort that a minority of the voters triumphed.

Another conclusion leaps to mind. The only safe, secure, and sure way of governing a people is to let them govern themselves. Those who felt the Constitution did not go far enough in this direction have been able through the years to make it more truly an instrument of democracy.

Our Constitution was written with the people of America in mind—this they would support, and that they would not. With or without the right to vote, the Americans had already shown that they would act when they were dissatisfied with government, and this was clearly in the minds of the framers of the Constitution. Throughout the years the Constitution has been changed by amendments, always in an attempt to put the will of the people into the law of the land.

Some political experts have drawn a triangle to show how a typical government works—the broad base of the triangle is the people, the central narrower section the legislative body, and the top peak the executive. In this triangle, the will of the executive is translated through the legislative to the people below.

A better representation of our form of government would be the same triangle with another one inverted above it—the one above would be the force of public opinion. We work through the executive and legislative branches of our government, but they are controlled by the irresistible force of public opinion.

Centuries ago, another small government was established in the country of Greece on much the same basis. The individual citizen was considered both worthy and capable of governing himself, and the Greeks gloried in this right. Franchise was not universal, individuals and groups were guilty of selfishness, self-interest, quarreling, conniving, and dishonesty, but on the foundation of individual dignity and right the Greeks created a civilization which still stands as a landmark in the history of mankind. During their era the fields of thought, logic, philosophy, and the arts rose to such heights that they are still a goal toward which we strive.

It was the proud boast of the Greeks that they lived under the rule of law and not of men. That was the step taken by our new country in its very beginning, and with us, as with the Greeks, the laws were made by men, and not by one man.

The first session of the new Congress passed the amendments to the Constitution which we know as our Bill of Rights—the laws of our land which guarantee our rights and freedoms as no other laws before them did for any people. These amendments were ratified by the states in 1791.

While it is true that much doubt and confusion as to the new government existed, we know that another attitude was even stronger, or it could not have been brought into being. Part of that attitude was a conviction that is as much a part of our heritage as the Constitution itself. That was the idea that the government might not be perfect, nor even nearly so, but that it could be changed by those who objected. Patrick Henry, who had refused to attend the Constitutional Convention, said, "My head, my hand and my heart shall be at liberty to retrieve the loss of liberty, and remove the defects of that system in a constitutional way."

There are always those among us who believe that "those people down in Washington" are ruining our country, but it is fortunate for us that most of us realize it is within our power to change what we do not like.

To balance the pessimism and uncertainty about the fate of the new government, there was an enthusiasm and faith in what was being attempted that was almost hysterical with joy.

Joseph Priestley, English scientist and friend of Benjamin Franklin, compared the Constitution with the English Revolution of 1689, which had merely replaced one royal dynasty with another. He said that America had formed a "completely new government on the principles of equal liberty and the rights of man." Others expected that the new government would be stronger than any of those in the Old World because it was more just and free.

To many wise and liberty-loving people, the new American government proved, by its very existence, that a large country could be ruled without monarchy or aristocracy, that religious worship could be permitted without restrictions, that people will obey a mild and equitable government better than a harsh and biased one, and (an important point, considering the situation in many countries) "that it was not a dangerous experiment to admit the Jews to all the privileges of natural-born citizens."

So it was that a new idea about how a land might be ruled came into being in a new country, and our government was established and began to function. No one knew what would happen, and there were many things to worry about—the national government had assumed a large debt, it had to find a source of income, and almost everything it did was for the first time, without historical precedent to set an example.

George Washington wrote to a friend that "my movements to the chair of government will be accompanied by feelings not unlike those of a culprit, who is going to the place of his execution." He knew from his experience that there is nothing more difficult than trying to work in an orderly and progressive manner with a varied assortment of people of all kinds, and that the way before him would be trying. Had he been made king, instead of President, it might have been so much easier—but he himself had upheld the right of people to have a voice in the government, and his devotion to our country proved his belief in this principle.

He believed, as did many others, that the experiment begun in America would come to change the face of the world and the structure of other governments.

Both of his attitudes were right—he underwent all of the problems of being the head of the new government, and he saw it begin its climb to greatness.

Chapter 7

WHO SHALL BE PRESIDENT?

The vote for George Washington for President showed there was no doubt in the minds of the Electors as to the right person for the job. He stood first in the country because of what he had already done for it and because of the trust people had in him.

The choice today is a much more difficult one. How do we know, out of the millions of people in America, which one will be the best for this vital position? This is the real cause of all the confusion and complexity of our presidential elections.

Do we want a rich man or a poor man, a thinker or a man of action? Would a professional politician who has held elected office most of his adult life know the ins and outs of government better, or would we do well to elect an amateur who would have no obligation to party or group?

The framers of the Constitution did not anticipate all of these questions, but the matter of the executive branch of the government worried them considerably. It took them three days to decide how many chief executives we should have, how he (or they) should be elected, and who would do it.

Many felt that having one chief executive would be too much like having a king. Others thought that the national legislature (which we call the Congress) should appoint "one or more chief executives, as experience might dictate." Edmund Randolph of Virginia thought there should be three chief executives —one from the North, one from the South, and one from the middle states. The final vote showed seven states for one chief executive, three against it.

Only a minority thought the President should be voted for by the people. Besides a general mistrust of the wisdom of the people at large, there were other good reasons against giving them this power. The states with the largest populations would invariably carry the election, someone pointed out, and the smaller states would not be allowed a voice in the selection of a President. Another item was that so many people lived so far apart without good roads or other means of communication they could hardly know enough about the candidates to vote intelligently. They would have to vote for someone of whom they had heard, which might lead to chaos—many votes split among many candidates.

On the first vote, nine states opposed popular election, and only one supported it. The decision was made when the Electoral College was proposed, which would allow popular representation from each state on the same basis as their representation in Congress. To avoid having each elector vote only for candidates from his own state, the third paragraph of Section 1 of Article II was written into the Constitution: each elector was to vote for two people, one of whom should not be an inhabitant of the same state as himself.

It was left to the various states to determine how these electors were to be chosen, and it was not until after the Civil War that all states chose them by general election.

George Washington, until after his election, belonged to no political party, because such a thing did not exist. He was an American and had been a supporter of the Revolution, instead of a Tory who supported the crown, and Americans had not yet divided into the groups we call political parties. After his election, those who favored a strong central government with a loose interpretation of the Constitution were called Federalists. Their opponents, such as Jefferson, supported the Constitution, but wanted it interpreted strictly according to the letter. They came to be called Republicans.

We expect the President who is elected today to be either a Democrat or Republican, and he probably will be because those are the two largest political parties. However, this does not necessarily mean what it seems to. Being a member of a political party in America can be a very flexible thing.

During the Revolution our country was divided into those who supported the crown and those who wanted independence: these differences were obviously very great. A man who was supporting the government of England and a man who was in rebellion against it could not work together to achieve their aims.

There are those in America today who are violently partisan: people who support the policies and candidates of one party, regardless of anything else. There are many who vote for a specific issue or candidate, regardless of party. In between are a majority of our citizens who think of themselves as Republicans or Democrats and almost always vote that way.

What does it mean to be a Republican or Democrat? In our country it means as much as the individual wishes it to mean. A man is called a "registered" Democrat or Republican because he has listed himself that way when he registered to vote. In some states, in the primary elections, he is given a ballot only for his party and so can vote only for its candidates. In others, ballots are non-partisan, so the voter can register a choice for a candidate in either party. In other elections, all ballots are non-partisan, so everyone may vote any way he chooses. He can vote a straight party ticket, or he may split his vote between candidates of each party. (He cannot vote for opposing candidates for the same office, of course, but he may well vote for a President from one party and a senator from another.)

In the Massachusetts state elections of 1962, for example, the Democrats made a clean sweep except for one state office, that of Attorney General. Edward Brooks, elected to that office, is a Republican and the first Negro in America to be Attorney General of any state. Obviously many voters split their tickets in this election.

Party membership in America, then, may consist of no more than a preference indicated at the time of registration. Neither major party collects dues from its members, and nineteen out of twenty American families make no financial contribution to the political party of their choice. Some people take their party loyalty very seriously, and some do not. In either case, no one in America is forced to belong to one party or another, or to vote for it if he does belong.

Since there are more registered Democrats than Republicans in our country currently, we would have nothing but Democratic Presidents if every registered party member voted.

How much does party affiliation mean to a presidential candidate? Normally, it means a great deal—it means that he believes as his party believes on domestic and foreign issues, that he has worked faithfully for his party, and that he can expect the support of most of its members. As with everything else connected with politics in America, though, there are exceptions to this rule.

When Ulysses S. Grant became a Republican candidate for the presidency, he had voted only once for a President, and that once for a Democrat. When Dwight D. Eisenhower was being discussed as a possible presidential candidate there was some confusion as to which party he belonged to.

Theodore Roosevelt was a Republican President, but he later bolted the party and helped form and led the Progressive party—which, however, did not win the presidential election.

A presidential candidate today, then, does not necessarily have to belong to one party or another in order to win. Are there any other qualifications he must have, except those required by the Constitution?

Before the election of John F. Kennedy as President, authorities on the political situation in America agreed generally on what seemed the obvious qualifications necessary for successful candidate. He should be a Protestant of North European descent in his fifties with an attractive wife and at least two children. He should be governor of a large northern state, especially one which was not predominantly either Democratic or Republican. He should not be obviously tied to any one element, such as labor or farmers or vested interests, and not outstandingly wealthy. Kennedy lacked a number of these requirements.

He was a Catholic, considerably under fifty, with one child, extremely wealthy, and not a governor but a senator. The voters of America are often apt to confuse the experts.

In the first years of our country, the Presidents were chosen from among those who had helped form our government—Washington, Adams, Jefferson, and Madison. The national idea of a President was a prominent and brilliant man, superior to most, and dedicated above all else to the welfare of the country. However, there were many who thought of Thomas Jefferson as the wildest sort of radical and predicted that his ideas would bring ruin to the country. (Washington himself was publicly attacked during his second term. Newspapers called him a tyrant, a dictator, and an impostor.)

When Andrew Jackson was elected, we had an entirely different type of President. A "man of the people," he was a soldier and poorly educated. (One historian says that he spelled Europe "Urop" and believed that the world was flat.)

In the wake of Jackson came a popular trend toward the "log-cabin" candidate and it was believed that a background of poverty was a great asset to a politician.

This had an interesting result in the campaign of 1840, when the Whig party nominated William Henry Harrison to run against the incumbent Martin Van Buren. The two had opposed each other in 1836, and Van Buren had won with 762,678 votes to 548,007 for Harrison.

Harrison was the son of a signer of the Declaration of Independence, wealthy, well educated, and had held a number of prominent offices before his nomination. During the campaign of 1839 an opposition newspaper quoted a supporter of Van Buren who said that if Harrison were given a pension of $2000 a year, a barrel of cider, and a log cabin, he would gladly retire from the presidential race.

Until this time the Whigs had had no particular party platform and had spent their time criticizing Van Buren. This quotation gave them a campaign theme. Party leaders marched through the streets carrying banners emblazoned with log cabins, drinking hard cider, and singing such songs as:

"Let Van from his coolers of silver drink wine,
And lounge on his cushioned settee.
Our man on his buckeye bench can recline,
Content with hard cider is he,
The iron-armed soldier, the true-hearted soldier
The gallant old soldier of Tippecanoe!"

In the subsequent election, Harrison won with a vote of 1,275,017 to Van Buren's 1,128,702. It was a year when everyone got fooled. The Whigs elected their candidate by presenting a picture that was not true to the facts, but their success was brief. President Harrison caught a cold which developed into pneumonia and he died a month after he took office. His Vice-President, John Tyler, took office (the first Vice-President to do so under those conditions), and the whole country knew that although Tyler had run on the Whig ticket his sentiments were more Democratic than Whig.

After the Civil War the most promising candidates were veterans of the Union forces, beginning with General Grant, but since the time of McKinley there has been no strong definite trend.

The high cost of presidential campaigns today has

begun to bring men with great wealth into this high office, and some feel that it may become impossible for anyone who is not a millionaire to run for President. In a way, this seems like a return to the early days of our country when only those distinguished by position, prestige, and possessions were even considered for the office. However, this trend was upset by the election of Jackson, and something may happen which will again make "the man of the people" the more popular candidate.

A presidential candidate today must be well known, he must want to be president, and he must convince the people that he is capable of solving the special problems faced by the country at the time. More than this, and the requirements listed in the Constitution, no one can say.

At different periods in our history we have elected Presidents who have not been outstanding, and at least two whose administrations saw a great deal of corruption. With the increased use of radio, television, newspapers, and magazines, it may begin to seem that the best use of advertising and public relations techniques will elect a President, regardless of his merits. This is especially interesting because it is a worry which is the exact opposite of one faced by the framers of the Constitution. We fear that a candidate may capitalize on charm and personality in order to win; they feared that the voters would have so little opportunity to come to know candidates that they might vote unwisely.

There are two factors in our way of life which help us vote for the right candidate; one is competition and the other is freedom of speech.

Before a candidate can win his party nomination, he must compete successfully with others in his party who want that honor. Anything known against him will be used by opponents in his own party, just as it is sure to be used against him in the presidential campaign by his opponent from the other party. A man who aspires to high office, then, must always guard against doing anything that may blot his record.

The factor of free speech may be even more important. If two of our Presidents were far from perfect, it is no secret from anyone. Every detail of their personal lives and their public administrations can be read by anyone who wishes. Sometimes mudslinging becomes too prominent in our political life, but its affirmative side, the right to tell the truth about everybody and everything, is priceless to us.

Chapter 8

FROM CAUCUS TO CONVENTION

If our founding fathers could look in on a modern political convention met to nominate a President, they would be astounded. Few things in our government have changed as much as the way in which presidential candidates are selected.

After the election of George Washington, it became a custom for members of each party who held seats in Congress to meet and decide on their candidates. The name for such a meeting was a caucus.

There was a great deal to be said for this system. The men in Congress understood how our government functioned and were able to decide which man would be best able to lead it. They could be held responsible for their choice because they held public office and were in the public eye.

On the other hand, if congressmen nominated

presidential candidates, was this not allowing the legislative section of the government to select the executive branch?

In the campaign of 1832 there was a public outcry against congressional caucuses. People began to say that it was too much like a closed shop, with only a few having a voice in the matter. In 1831 a group who opposed secret societies, calling themselves the "Anti-Masons," had formed a political party and held a convention in Philadelphia to nominate a presidential candidate.

The National Republicans and the Democrats both called national conventions to nominate their candidates, and the system with which we are familiar came into being.

Some feel that the conventions, which have been called a combination of a three-ring circus and a revival meeting, are not the right way to select a candidate for the presidency. They feel that there is too much political pressure, too much use of influence, and too much maneuvering to allow the average voter freedom of choice.

In an effort toward greater democracy, presidential primary elections were established in many states after 1900. The general purpose of the presidential primary was to allow the voters to elect delegates to the national political conventions and to indicate which presidential candidate they preferred. For a while more and more states adopted the primary system, but now the movement is on the decline. Ex-President Harry Truman called the presidential primaries "eyewash," and many people would agree with him.

One reason why primaries are not more effective is that less than a third of the states have them, and they are not uniform. In some states, voters may cast their ballots only for candidates of their own party; in other states they may vote for either party. Some states require their delegates to support the candidate selected by the primary and some do not.

All presidential candidates do not enter all primaries. In some states they may be voted for whether they have entered or not.

The most important reason why the primary system has proved ineffective is that it does not always affect the national convention.

Estes Kefauver, when working for the presidential nomination of his party, entered fifteen of the sixteen primaries in the United States, and won all but three of them. Out of 4,600,000 Democratic votes cast in these primaries, he won 3,140,000. Yet at the national convention he fell out of the race after the first two ballots. On the other hand, John F. Kennedy entered most of the presidential primaries in 1960 and his string of unbroken victories undoubtedly gave him strength in the national convention.

The primaries serve one purpose which is of prime importance to all those who hope to receive a party nomination at the convention. It helps put them in the public, and in the party, eye.

No party wants to nominate an obscure and little-known man because there is not enough time between the convention and the election to arouse enthusiasm for him among the voters. The candidate must thrust himself on the attention of the public in order to have a chance.

On the other hand, we have a tradition that he must not announce too early that he hopes to be a candidate. He must, as the saying goes, put himself in a prominent position and wait "for the lightning to strike."

A governor, for example, is mainly concerned with the problems in his own state, but if he has presidential ambitions he must make a reputation on a wider scale. He must inform himself of the issues of most interest to the country at large and begin to comment on them.

He may accept invitations to appear on television and radio and be interviewed for newspapers and magazines. Since so much depends on our international relations, he will probably travel abroad and begin to express opinions in that area.

As soon as a prospective candidate begins to make a name for himself, even on a local level, he begins to attract supporters. These supporters grow in number as he becomes more prominent and urge their friends to join them.

Supporters of a candidate may or may not be active politicians, but they must win the interest and enthusiasm of people at large if they wish for success. In order to be successful at a national convention, the candidate and his supporters must demonstrate that they represent what the people want.

There is a certain distrust in this country of professional politicians, but they are only as effective as we allow them to be. They cannot force or even persuade us to vote against our will and judgment, as long as we exercise these.

Right now there are hundreds of men in America, and very likely a number of women, who would like to be President. You cannot pick up a paper or magazine or listen to radio or watch television without learning about them, and about our government.

Once a candidate has been selected by his party, a tremendous campaign to show him in the best possible light will begin, but it is difficult to erase previous knowledge based on the facts.

Perhaps the best time to judge such a candidate is not during the campaign, but during his early history, which is almost always fully documented if we care to look.

Long before the national party conventions begin,

plans concerning them have started. Early in the winter before the summer in which the conventions will take place, the national committees meet in Washington and issue the calls for the conventions. The Republicans usually convene around the first of July and the Democrats a few weeks later.

The Democrats issue a statement as to the number of delegates each state may send. The Republicans give the number of candidates, the way in which their credentials may be forwarded, how contesting delegations shall submit their claims, and the process by which and the time within which the delegates may be chosen. These rules and requirements may be changed from election to election.

If delegates are not chosen in primary elections, they are chosen by district or state conventions. Each party has worked out what it considers the fairest representation for all its members throughout the nation.

The Democratic convention gives each state a number of convention delegates equal to twice its number of electors and gives each delegate one vote. A state with six representatives and two senators, for example, has eight electors—and sixteen votes in the national convention. Each party also allows a few delegates from the territories.

This would seem to be a fair system, except for one thing. Some states rarely, if ever, go Democratic in a national election. Should their delegates, then, be allowed equal votes with a state that will poll a huge Democratic majority? To make things more equitable, the Democrats allow four delegates-at-large from each state that went Democratic in the preceding national election.

The Democrats also have fractional votes in order to allow more delegates to attend the convention. A state may, for instance, send six full-vote delegates and four half-vote delegates, but the total number of votes must be that allowed by the national convention.

The Republicans allow four delegates-at-large from each state (two for each United States senator); two delegates-at-large for each congressman-at-large (a congressman chosen by the electorate of the entire state); a delegate from each congressional district that cast as many as 1000 votes for a Republican candidate in the last national election, and two delegates if as many as 10,000 Republican votes were cast; and each state that voted Republican in the last presidential election or subsequently elected a Republican to the United States Senate gets a bonus of six delegates. The principal territories and the District of Columbia are given from one to six delegates each.

Many of these delegates in both parties serve year after year, but changes are made as the party itself changes in the state. Being chosen is considered a very high honor, and so many people are eager to attend a national convention that official tickets are now engraved like bank notes so that they cannot be counterfeited.

A candidate for his party's nomination can find out some time in advance who the delegates from a certain state are apt to be. It is worth his time to meet them before the convention, or have one of his supporters meet them, to discuss his chances. (In the early days of our country it would have been more to the point to meet the electors.)

The city in which the convention is to be held is another matter for serious consideration. Local politicians will want it held in their own state in order to win more enthusiasm for local candidates, but the size of the city, the convenience of its hotels, newspapers, television stations, transportation, and other factors must be considered. Cities are so certain of a large upswing in business from the presence of a convention that they are willing to pay a large sum in order to attract one.

Chapter 9

ELEPHANTS AND DONKEYS

Each presidential hopeful tries to get in the center of the stage at his party convention. He and his followers establish a headquarters as prominently located as possible and make it a center of activity. One candidate held a fashion show in his quarters and had bathing beauties passing out pocket combs and chewing gum. Another had orange juice served by pretty girls, and one from Wisconsin had a 400-pound cheese for his visitors to eat.

This is window dressing. No candidate seriously thinks that he will win votes because his refreshments or entertainment are better than his opponents', but he wants to attract all the attention he can get.

A convention is loud and colorful, with uniformed bands and balloons and huge posters, pictures of candidates, bunting, pennants, badges, and a great deal of happy confusion. Watching it on television, one sometimes wonders how any business is conducted at all.

The convention itself is held in a huge auditorium —one large enough to hold up to 1700 delegates, the alternates who will take their places if necessary, the minor and major officials, from the chairman of the national committee to the doorkeeper and messengers, the representatives of newspapers, radio, and television, and 4000 to 5000 guests. Each state delegation is equipped with a standard—a long pole topped with a cardboard placard giving the name of the state— and has a microphone which will work only after the state has been formally recognized by the chair.

The convention is called to order by the chairman of the national committee, and the national anthem is sung. A rabbi, priest, or minister then gives the invocation, and a local official delivers a welcoming address. (If the local official is a presidential hopeful, the welcoming address may give his candidacy a big boost.)

The Call to the Meeting is read and the convention is under way. The main business of the first day is to set up the four main committees of the convention— those on credentials, permanent organization, rules, and resolutions.

One of the first things that must be done is to accredit the delegates. Sometimes two different party groups in the same state have elected delegates, each group pledged to a different candidate, and the Committee on Credentials must decide which to accredit. The decision may well mean defeat or victory for a candidate, so excitement runs high over the issue.

The very fact that this is possible gives one a better picture than anything else could of how politics works in America.

The people who nominate our President may be politicians or just plain citizens—their one distinguishing characteristic is that they care, and care very much, about who becomes President.

In one state there may be a group of the older and more conservative members of a political party, known as the "Old Guard." They have disagreed with the younger, more liberal members of the same party, and each group has met and elected its own delegates. Both groups go to the national convention, fully equipped with banners, placards, badges, and fighting spirit, equally determined to be recognized and vote for the candidate of their choice.

The Committee on Credentials must decide between them, and verbal fireworks are certain to follow.

If this seems evidence of a lack of order and a certain amount of confusion, it is also evidence that our way of electing a President is not rigidly shackled in rules and regulations. As long as change, difference of opinion, and discussion about procedures exist, our freedom of choice is safe.

Who are the delegates and the people who elect them? We can say, in all honesty, that they are the ruling class in America—but it is a class we all may join any time we wish.

We can join a political party and work for its ideas and projects, or we can try to develop new theories and activities within the party of our choice.

The keynote speech is given early in the convention by a prominent member of the party. He may be a presidential aspirant or not, and his speech may or may not help him. One promising candidate who gave a keynote speech in a convention succeeded in putting most of his listeners to sleep, and proved to even his most ardent supporters that he would not make a good nominee. A candidate communicates with the people during his campaign in many ways, but most of all through his speeches. In them he not only outlines his beliefs and policies, but expresses the sort of person he is.

The keynote speech has one main purpose. It is to arouse enthusiasm for the party and create harmony among its members.

One of the most astounding facts in the whole story of how we elect a President is that he is actually chosen by the party convention, and the campaign afterward is for the purpose of keeping those who support him interested enough to go to the polls.

Does that sound fantastic to you? Look at it this way. If every registered Democrat went to the polls at each election, and voted for his party, the Democratic candidates would win all national elections. There are more registered Democrats than there are Republicans at this time.

Republican candidates get elected when enough Republican voters go to the polls, and enough Democrats stay home. Since all the registered Democrats will never go to the polls in any one election, the Republicans can beat them if they can get enough of their party members out.

When the conventions are over, most voters have made up their minds and know how they will vote. The campaign itself may change very few votes. Its main purpose is to get the people whose minds are already made up to the polls.

This is such a staggering fact that we will return to it again. When the effort, activity, and money spent on each presidential campaign are considered, it is incredible to know that its purpose IS TO GET PEOPLE TO THE POLLS and not especially to change their opinions.

Not all Americans vote. This is the sad fact confronting every party convention. They know that their candidate will be like a gold miner, working on a stream rich with ore. He knows that all of the gold he needs is in the stream, but the problem is to get it out.

If either candidate could get every voter who favored him to the polls, he would be almost certain of victory.

The keynote speech, then, is to arouse the sort of enthusiasm which will last until the election. It is directed not only to the thousands of people at the convention, but to the millions who will hear it on television and read about it in newspapers and magazines.

The keynote speaker tries to make it clear, even before the candidate is nominated, that his party and his party alone will save our country from the perils which confront it. He paints his own party policies and history in glowing colors and explains the errors and evils of the other party.

During the second day of the convention, the real business is being conducted behind the scenes. In the auditorium itself there will be a varied program of speeches, music, introductions of well-known party members, and appearances of groups from throughout the country. The Committee on Permanent Organization makes its report, which includes the appointment of a permanent presiding officer for the convention.

This officer usually takes the floor and gives an address.

The Rules Committee makes its report, and this may arouse controversy. In the Democratic party it was once necessary to have a two-thirds vote for any candidate, which meant that southern delegates could, by banding together, prevent the nomination of a candidate they disliked. In 1936, Franklin Roosevelt and James Farley were able to change this to a simple majority rule, thus taking some of the power from the southern bloc. In 1940 the Democratic convention adopted a rule which gave four additional delegates-at-large to each state which had gone Democratic in the previous presidential election, thus restoring some of their authority to the southern states.

The next important project for the convention is the formulation of the party platform. This is a public statement of what the party believes, what it expects to accomplish, and how it expects to do it.

Since there are, in the same party, those who believe war can be avoided by a strong foreign-aid program and those who believe the opposite, people who believe the government must have greater authority over the states and those who believe just the opposite, and as many opposing viewpoints on every issue that arises, the construction of a party platform is difficult.

It must be broad enough to win the support of as many party members as possible and yet not radical enough to offend any. It must include the things that concern people, but it must avoid raising an issue which might lose the election.

In 1948 the Democratic convention adopted a strong civil-rights plank. This was a surprising move by a party which had so much to lose by such an open declaration. An example of a different approach to the issue was a platform plank relating to the Supreme Court and its decisions on segregation. In order to offend no one (and, on the other hand, please no one particularly), one year's plank read that the party "recognizes the Supreme Court of the United States as one of the three constitutional and coordinate branches of the Federal government" whose decisions "are part of the law of the land."

Like many other platform planks, this one meant much more than it said in words. Because there was so much dissension about the Supreme Court decisions on civil rights of Negroes in the South, the Democratic party was on the spot. If it upheld these decisions, it risked losing its southern votes. If it failed to mention the matter at all, it would lose the votes of liberals. The plank, then, sufficed—it referred to the matter without taking a strong stand on either side.

Harry Truman, Hubert Humphrey, and a few

other Democrats put up a big battle and got a strong civil-rights plank in the platform of the 1948 convention. When it was read, half of the Alabama and all of the Mississippi delegates walked out of the hall. However, the plank eventually won more votes for Truman in the North than it lost for him in the South.

During the Civil War, as the presidential election approached, the Democrats said in their platform that the war was a mistake and should be ended immediately. They chose as their candidate General George B. McClellan, former General-in-Chief of the Union Army. They believed that the vote of all those who were tired of the war, and especially of the soldiers who still felt devotion and loyalty to McClellan, would win them the victory. General McClellan refused to endorse the platform. In a public speech he said that he could not look in the faces of his gallant comrades and tell them that their sacrifices had been in vain.

Usually, however, a candidate goes along with his party platform, even if it is based on compromises which he does not like and omits issues which he thinks are important.

Writing the platform is usually begun months before the convention, and all sorts of pressure groups try to get certain things put in or left out. We are, again, inclined to think of pressure groups as contrary to the spirit of a democracy, but this may not be so. If, at the time, we had believed in Prohibition, we would have thought every group working for it was in the right and all those working against it in the wrong. A pressure group may be working for business interests or for more federal aid to education, but whatever its purpose it is simply a group of people who believe so strongly in something that they make an effort to get it. The way to change the effect of pressure groups is not to eliminate them, but to make use of the same technique for causes which we believe are worthwhile. A citizen who writes to his own congressman is a very small pressure group, just as is the organization of public-spirited people who petition Congress for more aid to any depressed group within our population.

Once the platform has been written and accepted, the convention is ready for its major business, which has already been the subject of furious debate behind the scenes. Who is going to be nominated for President?

Each candidate has secured the support of as many state delegates as possible and may know more or less how many votes he can expect when the balloting begins.

Perhaps he is eager to be the nominee, and yet he knows that he lacks enough support. In each convention there are a number of states that will cast their first ballots for "favorite sons," their governor or another prominent person. These votes are often not cast in the serious expectation that such a "favorite son" will win, and thus may be available to another candidate in later balloting. Each candidate will try to strengthen his cause with each state, and will also talk to some of his opponents.

If he is from a strong northern state, he may approach a candidate from a western or southern state and suggest that they combine forces. If one runs as President, the other as Vice-President, their combined appeal may give them much greater strength.

Or the candidate may feel, upon looking the situation over, that he has little chance of winning the prized nomination at this particular election. He can then approach a more popular candidate with an offer to throw in his own support in order to consolidate his chances for the future.

Harry M. Daugherty, campaign manager for Warren G. Harding, predicted five months before the convention in 1920 that "the convention will be deadlocked, and after the other candidates have gone their limit, some twelve or fifteen men, worn out and bleary-eyed from lack of sleep, will sit down, about two o'clock in the morning, around a table in a smoke-filled room in some hotel and decide the nomination.

When that time comes, Harding will be selected." In this case, the nomination came about as he thought, but the election was won more by indifference than enthusiasm. The amount of money spent on the campaign was small compared to others, and the percentage of voters who went to the polls was not great. Harding was put in office as much by the indifference of the voters as by the enthusiasm of those who supported him.

Americans who wish to be effective in selecting a President have many avenues open to them, and as long as those avenues are open they cannot truthfully blame anyone else for what happens.

They can make up their minds before their state primaries or party conventions and try to persuade as many of their friends and neighbors as possible to side with them. They can take an active part in their party activities so they know what is going on and help direct it in the way they think it should go. They can confer with the delegates from their state to try to influence the national convention.

Even after the nomination has been made by the convention, they can be effective by their votes. Although it is true that people make up their minds before the election, there is no law in our land which requires them to abide by it. A Republican who feels that his party has made a mistake is perfectly free to switch allegiance and work for the opposition candidate.

In the long run, it is not the party nor the convention nor the candidate that wins the election—it is the voters who care enough to go to the polls.

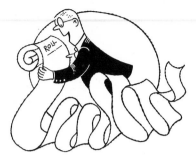

Chapter 10

THE BALLOTS BEGIN TO FLY

What has happened up to this time in the convention is necessary and important, and a prelude to the real business of the whole affair.

These thousands of people from all over America have convened to select a candidate—a man they hope will be the next President.

We have already mentioned the "smoke-filled" room," which is a part of the American legend about the nomination of Presidents. According to this legend, the successful candidate is selected by a few top party leaders in a private session.

Looking at the facts, it is difficult to see how this can be done without the consent of the people, given either willingly or by their indifference.

Long before the convention begins, primaries have been held in about a third of the states of the country.

While these primaries are not wholly successful in what they attempt to do, they provide an indication of popular sentiment.

Perhaps more important than the primaries, in recent years, have been the public opinion polls. Several firms have worked out ways of testing public opinion by asking a series of questions of a percentage of the people, and these polls are made use of by party leaders. In some cases, the polls have been wrong, but generally they show what sort of man the voters want and what issues they consider most important.

No party leaders, regardless of their influence, would be so stupid as to promote a candidate who cannot win votes. They may, as in the case of Woodrow Wilson, select a candidate known to be popular and whom they believe will follow orders when he is in office. And, as in the case of President Wilson, they may find that their candidate has a mind of his own and will do what he believes is right when he is in office.

Many authorities have outlined the qualities they believe a successful candidate must have, but the most vital of them is the ability to win votes. This means, again, that it is the voter of America who makes the final decision, and the successful party is the one which most clearly reads the will of the people.

What sort of man do we want for President? As was said before, this changes from election to election, and even the experts can give only educated guesses. They generally agreed (before the 1960 election when forty-three-year-old John F. Kennedy, a Catholic, became President) on the following set of requirements:

1. A man of unblemished personal integrity. The American people are broad-minded, but a man whose record is flawed will be attacked by his own party members, as well as by members of the opposition. Anyone who is ambitious to be President recognizes this and, since such ambition usually begins long before a hoped-for nomination, keeps it as a guide to his conduct.

2. A man who *wants* to be President. While we tend to distrust the obvious pusher, the man who is too aggressive in his desire for prominence, it would be foolish to elect someone who had no desire to fill such a high office. Being President is difficult work, demanding much of anyone who attempts it. Only someone to whom it is greatly worthwhile and by whom it is deeply desired would be suitable for the office.

3. A man in good health and with the ability to campaign, about fifty three years old. Because of the demands made on the time and energy of the President, only a man in good health seems suitable for the office. A very pronounced energy and determina-

tion overcame this to some extent in the case of Franklin Roosevelt, who had been a victim of polio.

The ability to campaign is a quality harder to define. Candidates are now brought so much closer to the voters through the media of television, radio, magazines, and newspapers that a charming personality would seem to be a rigid requirement. The question is what sort of personality most voters will find acceptable. Some people are pleased by friendliness, informality, and warmth, while some feel that a President should be dignified, sedate, and less approachable. There is a strong belief that a sense of humor can be a liability in a candidate, but we must remember that Abraham Lincoln is almost as well known for his jokes and funny anecdotes as for his statesmanship. Certainly, people have voted through the years for men of widely different personalities.

4. A man from a heavily populated or doubtful state, especially one east of the Mississippi. The more population a state has, the more electoral votes it commands: hence, a candidate who can carry the most electoral votes in his own state has a better chance. If the state goes Republican in some elections and Democratic in others, a native son may win it in an election and thus bring in votes that might otherwise be doubtful.

The Republicans would not be apt to select a candidate from Georgia, which always goes Democratic, nor would the Democrats choose a man from a state which always goes Republican.

The number of electoral votes in the East makes a candidate from that section of the country more desirable. Only Hoover, Eisenhower, and Truman have been successful candidates from west of the Mississippi though the growth of California may change this picture soon.

5. A man with a record of public service, and most especially a lawyer. Americans want a President who cares more about the welfare of the country than anything else, and a man whose record shows this concern has a head start. A man who had every other desirable qualification but had never shown enough interest in public concerns to hold local offices, work for good causes, sponsor worthwhile enterprises, or do anything for anyone except himself, would seem a very dubious candidate to the people.

If lawyers are nominated more than any other profession, it is probably because this choice of career indicates that a man is interested in our government and its laws and takes part in public life.

6. There are three qualifications that vary with the person and do not necessarily apply to every election. A party which has a President in office will almost always nominate him again. (The 22nd amendment to the Constitution, passed in 1947, limits the Presi-

dent to two terms.) If it did not, it would be like admitting that its policy and its President, were wrong.

A man who has once run for President and been defeated is not considered a very promising candidate, though some men have run more than once for the office. William Henry Harrison won on his second try; Thomas E. Dewey failed both times.

A member of a minority group does not have a very good chance of becoming President. Party leaders realize that if a very brilliant, capable, and dedicated person were a Jew, a woman, a Moslem, a Negro or a member of some other minority group, a large number of voters would tend to think of him in that way rather than as an individual. They would not vote for or against his ability, but as they felt about the group to which he belonged. However, the voters elected a Catholic in 1960, though some experts predicted it could never happen, and this is one of the phases of our national life that is continually changing.

It is interesting to note that we have had Presidents from only fourteen states: Kentucky, North Carolina, Pennsylvania, Virginia, Massachusetts, New Hampshire, South Carolina, New York, Ohio, Vermont, New Jersey, Iowa, Missouri, and Texas. To date, Virginia and Ohio are in the lead, with eight Presidents from Virginia and seven from Ohio.

With all this in mind, the convention approaches the task of nominating a candidate. Even though the requirements for a candidate seem great, each party may have as many as a dozen men who meet all of them. Primaries and public opinion polls will have indicated which are the stronger, but a final selection must be made.

The roll of states is called, and, as each state is called in turn, the chairman of its delegation may make a nominating speech. These speeches may last for fifteen or twenty minutes, but one of the most famous, and shortest, in history was twenty-six words.

The Democratic convention had met in Charleston, South Carolina, in 1860 to nominate a presidential candidate. Swords were drawn between the northern and southern sections of the party, and a fierce battle over the platform took place. It ended when the southern delegates withdrew after fifty seven ballots, with no candidate receiving the necessary two-thirds of the votes. The convention closed, reconvened later, and still could not agree. The southern Democrats withdrew, and the northern section remaining, nominated Stephen A. Douglas. The southern Democrats held a convention of their own and nominated John C. Breckinridge.

The Republicans met for their convention in Chicago, and sentiment was split between Abraham

Lincoln and William H. Seward. Norman B. Judd rose to his feet and said, "I desire, on behalf of the delegation from Illinois, to put in nomination, as a candidate for President of the United States, Abraham Lincoln, of Illinois."

Delegate Burton Cook, from Ottawa, took his handkerchief out of his pocket, a signal for which Lincoln supporters had been waiting, and the hall was instantly filled with a loud outcry for the man from Illinois. It lasted until Cook returned his handkerchief to his pocket.

When voting began, Seward had $173\frac{1}{2}$ votes and Lincoln 102 on the first ballot. On the second ballot, Lincoln had 181 and Seward $184\frac{1}{2}$.

In the balloting at national conventions, the first vote is not always as important as the second one. A candidate who does not make a big gain on the second ballot (if the competition is great) has usually begun to lose. In this case, both candidates gained, but Lincoln gained more and showed which way the tide was running. On the third ballot, Lincoln had $231\frac{1}{2}$ of the whole 465 and Seward had only 180. Immediately other states asked to change their votes and a final total of 364 were cast for Lincoln.

In the 1952 Democratic convention, Estes Kefauver, who had won all but three of the fifteen primaries he had entered, got 340 votes on the first ballot. When he picked up only $22\frac{1}{2}$ votes on the second ballot, it was clear that he was not going to win.

In the Republican convention of that same year, Eisenhower got 595 votes on the first ballot out of a necessary 614—immediately Minnesota asked permission to switch, and so many other states followed that his victory was assured.

During the roll call, when each state is allowed a nominating speech, many candidates are nominated who do not expect a victory. A state may have a "favorite son," whose nomination is merely an honor paid to him and which no one takes very seriously. Other people may be nominated as an indication that they are to be considered prominent in the party and will be heard from in the future.

Some state delegations have been instructed as to how they are to vote before coming to the convention. They may or may not be required to stay with a certain candidate until he releases them to vote otherwise. The "unit rule" requires that all delegates from a certain state vote for the same candidate, but the Republican convention does not enforce this rule, and the Democrats do only when a delegation has been specifically instructed to observe it.

Therefore, the votes on the first ballot are often scattered and do little more than indicate which way the wind is blowing. Each candidate hopes for a huge demonstration or a deadlock over two opposing candidates which will work in his favor.

In the Democratic convention of 1852, the problem was to find a candidate who would appeal to both the North and the South. The most prominent contenders were Lewis Cass, William L. Marcy, James Buchanan, and Stephen A. Douglas. No one of them could win enough votes, and so the nomination went to Franklin Pierce, a brilliant and charming lawyer from New Hampshire, who, if he was little known, at least had few bitter enemies. When informed of his nomination, he is reported to have said, "Gentlemen, you are looking at the most surprised man in the world."

At the Democratic convention of 1868, the party was not so successful in its "dark horse" candidate. Unable to decide between Thomas Hendricks of Indiana and General Winfield Scott Hancock of Pennsylvania, the convention nominated Horatio Seymour, its chairman.

Seymour was so overcome by the honor that he said, "Gentlemen, I thank you, and may God bless you for your kindness to me, but your candidate I cannot be." He later changed his mind, but was defeated by General Grant.

If a state delegation does not wish to nominate anyone, it may yield that honor to another state, or it may second a nomination already made.

The language of nominating speeches is often flowery and impassioned, since this is an opportunity to arouse enthusiasm for a candidate. Joseph Scott, when he nominated Herbert Hoover for a second term in 1932, said, "Babylon and Nineveh and ancient Rome wallowed in the wealth of material prosperity, stood naked and unashamed in their perdition—and succumbed."

Colonel Robert G. Ingersoll's nominating speech for James G. Blaine is usually considered the high point of nominating oratory. "Like an armed warrior", he said, " like a plumed knight, James G. Blaine marched down the halls of the American congress and threw his shining lance full and fair against the brazen forehead of every traitor to his country and every maligner of his fair reputation." Blaine was known, after that, to his supporters as "the Plumed Knight," but his opponents called him "the Tattooed Man."

Alfred E. Smith, the Democratic candidate in 1928, got his campaign nickname, "the Happy Warrior," from the nominating speech made on his behalf by Franklin D. Roosevelt, who said, "We offer one who has the will to win—who not only deserves success but commands it. Victory is his habit—the happy Warrior, Alfred Smith."

Chapter 11

HOW MANY BALLOTS?

The most exciting part of a national convention is
the balloting. No matter what has gone on before,
no matter how strong each candidate appears to be,
the real test is in the votes of the delegates.

When the party holding the convention has a President in office, he almost invariably receives the nomination on the first ballot. One time this did not happen
when the Whigs elected William Henry Harrison
in 1840. Harrison died a month after taking office
and was succeeded by John Tyler, whom the Whigs
repudiated in 1844. Tyler had not been a President
to their liking, and they nominated another candidate.

About half of the time, the convention nominates
its candidate on the first ballot, but in 1924 the Democrats balloted 100 times in sixteen days without any

candidate receiving a majority. On the 103rd ballot, John W. Davis received the nomination.

We can step back to the Republican convention of 1884 to witness a demonstration that set the pattern for those so typical of a convention today. Those who support certain candidates do everything possible to arouse enthusiasm for their choice, and one excellent device is to have it appear that such enthusiasm is already so great it cannot be restrained.

Feeling was running high in this particular convention. James G. Blaine was a popular candidate, but the reformers in the party opposed him strenuously because they believed he had been involved in unsavory financial deals. Though his campaign nickname was "the Plumed Knight," his opponents thought he was exactly the opposite.

One of Blaine's followers suggested that each delegate should pledge his support to the nominee in advance of the nomination, and this aroused even greater protest.

Blaine, who was never elected President, seemed to be extremely fortunate in the oratory of those who nominated him. At this convention one of his supporters rose to his feet and said, "Nominate him and the campfires and beacon lights will illuminate the continent from the Golden Gate to Cleopatra's Needle. Nominate him and the millions who are now waiting will rally to swell the column of victory that is sweeping on."

As soon as he mentioned Blaine's name, a shout arose from the hall, which almost took the roof off the building. Delegates leaped to their feet, tore banners from the walls, and danced and paraded through the auditorium. This is sometimes called the first actual "demonstration"at a political convention, but there was certainly something similar, and planned, when Lincoln was nominated.

On the first ballot, Blaine received $334\frac{1}{2}$ votes, and his other two opponents 278 and ninety three respectively. On the fifth ballot, Blaine won the nomination.

In the convention of 1876, Ingersoll had given the rousing nomination for Blaine quoted before, the one which won him the nickname of "the Plumed Knight." Immediately after the speech, an enemy of Blaine's cut the main gas pipe and put out all the lights in the hall. This prevented voting, and by the next morning the opponents of Blaine had managed to dampen enthusiasm for him, so that a compromise candidate was nominated.

Even while the balloting is taking place, a great deal is going on behind the scenes. If three candidates are strong contenders for the nomination, pulling a fairly equal number of votes, the advisers of two of them may try to work out an agreement. If they combine forces, one deciding to accept the nomination for Vice-President, their total may come to a majority. (Few strong candidates are willing to settle for a vice-presidential nomination in place of the top spot, but it's always worth a try.)

The delegates who have nominated and voted for a "favorite son" will eventually vote for a prominent candidate. Every leading contender tries to get their support.

Unless the unit rule of voting has been required by the state convention, delegates from any one state may split their votes. Eight may be for one candidate, six for another, and two for still another. Frequently state delegations hold informal caucuses in the midst of balloting, each group trying to persuade the others to change their votes.

All of this maneuvering and persuasion may seem to be the use of undue influence, the attempt to force the will of a certain group on the entire convention. On the other hand, we must remember that it is also the exercise of the rights of individuals and minorities to work for what they believe is right. As Associate Chief Justice William Douglas said, "The democratic process is an opportunity for the truth to evolve."

Out of the all the confusion, discussion, and bargaining, the one candidate on whom all will agree eventually emerges. Once he has been nominated, he must still win the votes of the people. His own party members, if they do not approve of him, may vote for his opponent in the actual election, or they may lessen his chances by staying home from the polls and not voting at all.

The "demonstrations" at conventions have been criticized by many, and there is a feeling that they should be abolished. The supporters of each candidate try to make their own demonstration the loudest and longest, and each is carefully clocked to see how long it lasts. Obviously each group uses every device in its power, and some of the demonstrations are quite clearly planned and carefully carried out. Fortunately, Americans have seen so much of advertising and public relations techniques that they are able to use their own judgment as to how much is real and how much is contrived.

Once the presidential candidate has been nominated, the vice-presidential candidate must be selected. As our elections for these high offices were originally planned, the Vice-President was the candidate who received the second highest number of votes by the electors. Thus, when John Adams became our second President, Thomas Jefferson became Vice-President, the only time these offices were held by men of opposing parties.

The Twelfth Amendment to the Constitution,

proposed in 1803 and ratified in 1804, provided that both the President and Vice-President should be elected, thus removing the possibility that they could again be of opposing parties.

The vice-presidency has been called the least important office in America, but this is hardly true. A number of Vice-Presidents have later been elected President, and seven of them have become President through the death of the incumbent. These were John Tyler, Millard Fillmore, Andrew Johnson, Chester Alan Arthur, Theodore Roosevelt, Calvin Coolidge, and Harry Truman.

Usually the presidential candidate selects his running mate, but sometimes it is done by the party on the basis of compromise. If the presidential candidate is from one section of the country, the Vice-President may be selected from another; if the President represents one element of the party, the Vice-President may be selected to represent another. It is always hoped that the vice-presidential candidate will help bind the party more closely together and attract votes that the presidential candidate might not win by himself.

With the two candidates selected, the convention is practically finished, and in a way the election is already decided. Some experts believe that ninety per cent of the voters know, at the end of the national convention, which candidate they favor. The ten per cent who are undecided are not enough to make a victory for either side, unless enough of the other voters stay home from the polls on Election Day.

Presidential campaigns, then, which are among the colorful activities of the democratic process, go into action immediately after the conventions to get the voters to the polls.

Chapter 12

SHAKING HANDS
WITH THE VOTERS

If a presidential candidate could, he would shake hands with every member of his party during the campaign. He realizes, much more than most of us do, how important each single vote can be.

Americans will vote the party ticket because they believe in the party, but they will bother to go to the polls only when they believe deeply in the candidate.

Political experts believe that about seventy-five per cent of the voters in America are members of one major party or the other by inheritance, conviction, or environment. Perhaps the family has always belonged to a certain party, perhaps it is the things for which it stands which have led to the loyalty, or perhaps current conditions have led to the decision. (During the Depression, the Democrats gained many converts because of the policies of Franklin D. Roosevelt. In the midterm election of 1866, the radicals who hated the South were able to overthrow moderate policies toward the reconstruction of that section after the Civil War, and the era of "carpetbagging" began. For twenty years the Republicans held the presidency, but this period united the South into what is called the "solid South," a large bloc of Democratic votes, which hasn't changed much to this day.

Although we say that the election of the President is already decided in the minds of the voters by the end of the conventions, this does not mean that his election is assured. One recent election proved the truth of this.

When the Democrats convened in 1948, many of the delegates wore large badges which said, "We're Just Mild About Harry," an indication that Truman's popularity with his own party was not overwhelming. He received the nomination, but not the wholehearted support of all Democrats. Those in charge of party funds were not inclined to make a huge investment in his campaign, which many of them were convinced would be a failure.

The polls made it perfectly clear that Thomas E. Dewey would be elected President, and only a few disagreed with them. Among those few were some who began asking questions of the voters. A sample conversation might go like this: "Who do you think will be elected President?" "Dewey." "And whom will you vote for?" "Me? I'm going to vote for Truman." The conviction began to grow among Truman's supporters that there was a strong "grassroots" enthusiasm for him. In other words, the gold was in the creek, waiting to be panned by a good miner.

Truman mapped out a campaign without the promise of adequate money to finance it or enough support from his party to make it worth-while. He is reported to have told his campaign manager, "I expect to travel all over the country and talk at every whistle stop. We are going to be on the road most of the time from Labor Day to the end of campaign. It's going to be tough on everybody, but that's the way it's got to be . . ."

He was as good as his word. With his campaign train he began to tour the country, stopping frequently to talk with the people who had gathered to hear him. Not all of the crowds were large, and the ones which were did not convince everyone that he was a popular candidate. "People will go to look at a live President," it was said, "but it doesn't mean they'll vote for him."

Near Oklahoma City, the funds to pay for the train ran out. An emergency meeting was held on the train, and Oklahoma Democrats contributed enough to keep the campaign going.

Truman was a fighter, and he pulled no punches in his speeches. He had made a clear issue of civil rights, which he knew would lose him many votes of those whom he labeled the "Dixiecrats." To make up for this loss, he campaigned heavily in the farm areas of the Middle West, stirring up sentiment against the Republican party. Dewey, who was sure he had strong farm support, avoided the area.

On election night, the polls were positive of a Dewey victory, and the early returns substantiated this belief. Many Americans went to bed that night, convinced that Dewey was President, and did not find out until the next morning that Truman had won.

Truman had a popular margin of 2,135,747 votes, but 23,300 of them would have given Dewey the victory. These votes, however, would have had to be in California, Illinois, and Ohio, three states with large electoral votes that Truman carried with a very small margin.

During his campaign, Truman covered 22,000 miles and made 275 talks. Is this the secret of winning an election? Wendell Willkie traveled 28,000 miles and made 540 talks—and lost. William Jennings Bryan made 630 speeches—and lost.

The candidate and other leaders of each party map out the campaign, deciding how best to use their money and time to win the election.

The matter of money is a difficult one. Both of the

major parties receive funds only from contributions, since they have no membership dues, and they never have as much as they need. (As Will Rogers said, "It costs a lot of money even to get beat.")

The national committee of each party is allowed to spend only $3,000,000 on a single campaign, but in 1956 the Republicans spent nearly $4,000,000 and the Democrats close to $3,000,000 for television and radio. The extra money is raised and spent by independent agencies who favor the candidate, and each of these agencies is also allowed to spend $3,000,000. It would be hard to say, therefore, exactly how much is spent on any one presidential campaign.

The expenditure of time requires a sense of timing and good judgment. The leaders know which states have the most electoral votes, and they also know that their chances of winning some of these states are so slim it is useless to campaign there. However, Eisenhower made a whirlwind trip through southern states, which are traditionally Democratic, and won Virginia, Florida, and Texas. Four years later he added Louisiana to the fold.

When a campaign is planned, local party leaders are alerted to help with the program in their own areas. Any time and place where a large group of people will be gathered together for some purpose provides a ready-made audience for a speech. Candidates attend state fairs, dedicate airports, and lead state rallies. They make a point of meeting publicly with local candidates for state or national offices, to show party unity and lend their support.

One of the most effective, though the most difficult, parts of campaigning is the "whistle-stop." Every mile of the trip that a candidate will take is carefully mapped out by campaign managers to include as many brief speeches as possible. These not only stir up the voters, but provide good publicity material.

Local party leaders contend vigorously for the honor of having their candidate stop at THEIR town, at THEIR county fair, at THEIR crossroads, or at THEIR high school carnival. A candidate who speaks briefly to a group of high school students may not get any votes from them, but his picture in the newspapers will show that he has an interest in the young people of our country.

Before each stop, the candidate must not only rehearse what he will say, but must also become familiar with the names of local notables and high points of the region's history. References to some well-known resident and the area history will win him enthusiasm and show that he is well versed in things that interest the voters.

Each candidate will make a number of "major" speeches during his campaign, explaining the issues involved and declaring his sentiments, and these speeches receive wide publicity. He will also make television appearances, carefully planned and rehearsed, to reach people who might not otherwise hear him. As with every new element that has entered the history of campaigning, there are many who think the use of television will lead to the election of totally unsuitable men for President. They feel that the qualities which make a man effective on television are not necessarily those which would make a good President, and there is truth in this attitude. However, it is also true that the more people see and hear of a candidate, the better they should be able to judge him.

The presidential candidate cannot make all of the speeches or meet all of the people necessary to secure his election. Other party leaders and members must do their share.

A colorful part of elections that once swayed many votes is now almost discarded. This was the torchlight parade.

Some time during the campaign, the party members of a town, either Democratic or Republican, would plan a huge parade and rally in support of their candidate. If Republican, all party members in town would be asked to join the parade and light their houses in honor of the event.

In New England, many small towns had drill teams which wore distinctive uniforms and represented their towns in such affairs. They, too, would be invited to attend the parade and rally.

Everyone in town, regardless of party, took part— either to march in the parade or watch it from the sidewalks. There would be bands and banners and brilliantly glowing torches and the drill teams in colorful uniforms. Each marcher, in many towns, carried both a torch and a tin cup.

As the parade made its way through the streets, it approached houses with lighted candles in the windows, signifying that those who lived there were members of the party holding the rally. The leader of the parade would halt, call his followers to attention, and give the order, "Three cheers for the house on the left!" In some cases, if the home owner had an attractive daughter, he might have her posed in a front window, wearing a white robe and holding the American flag, as the Spirit of Liberty.

Parades usually ended at the town common, near the town hall. Sometimes schoolchildren would present a tableau illustrating one of the great party principles or historic events, each child holding a lighted candle.

Speeches were given at the town hall, but before they began, the tin cups came into use. Cider and doughnuts were served to one and all to strengthen them for the several hours of campaign oratory that might ensue.

Such events not only illustrated the deep interest people took in politics, but stimulated it, just as campaign tactics do today.

At one point or another during the campaign, the "mudslinging" begins. This consists of attempts to ruin the opposing candidate by starting discrediting stories about him. When Alfred E. Smith, the first Catholic to run for President as a major party candidate in America, was campaigning, various stories about his religious loyalties were circulated. One of the most astonishing of these was that a tunnel was being dug from the Vatican to America, and that upon Smith's election the Pope would begin ruling the United States.

Mudslinging is never admirable, but we can congratulate ourselves that it is neither as vicious nor as effective as it has been in the past. John C. Fremont, when a candidate, was attacked as a free-love advocate, a drunkard, and a Puritan prohibitionist. Franklin Pierce was accused of being a drunkard, of being opposed to Catholics, and of having a daughter who was a nun. (Like most Americans of his time, Pierce drank, but he also headed a local temperance group; he had fought hard for the rights of Catholics to hold office in New Hampshire, where it was unconstitutional, and he had no daughters at all.) George Washington was called a tyrant and a dictator who should be hurled from his throne, and it was said of him, "If ever a nation was debauched by a man, the American nation was debauched by Washington."

Sometimes an emotional attack on personal creed, race, or religion backfires. When James C. Blaine (certainly an unfortunate candidate) was running for office in 1884, he dozed while a speech was being made on his behalf at a meeting held by a group of ministers. One of them referred to the opposing party, the Democrats, as the party of "Rum, Romanism and Rebellion." Otherwise he might have repudiated the statement before it got into the newspapers and infuriated the Roman Catholics. Blaine lost New York with its thirty-six electoral votes, and the election by what has been called one of the worst blunders in any presidential campaign.

Campaign slogans are effective if they capture the imagination of the people, and some of them have become part of our language. McKinley's "A Full Dinner Pail" and Hoover's "A Chicken in Every Pot" made a universal appeal to a human need, and "Happy Days Are Here Again" and "He Kept Us Out of War" encouraged many votes.

No item, and no device, is so humble that it does not find a use in a presidential campaign. Pictures of candidates and their slogans appear on match folders, tiny sewing kits, lumps of sugar, potholders, bumper stickers, posters, and banners. Party members are encouraged to send letters or post cards to their friends urging them to vote for the right candidate, and telephone campaigns are considered one of the most effective methods of arousing interest.

Every party leader and member is urged to "get on the band wagon" and stir up interest. Every voter, no matter how lukewarm or how far he lives from the polls, is to be contacted and urged to vote.

A presidential campaign should convince our country, every four years, that the individual voter is the most important person in America.

Chapter 13

HOW WE VOTE

Perhaps $100,000,000 was spent in the presidential campaign of 1956 to persuade the voters to go to the polls.

Yet forty million people of voting age did not use their vote. About 7,000,000 of these were probably southern Negroes who, in one way or another, are prevented from voting. Six million were people who had moved recently and had not established residence in their new homes (or applied for absentee ballots). About 5,000,000 were sick (and had not applied for absentee ballots). Two and seven-tenths million were traveling (and had not applied for absentee ballots). Perhaps two and five-tenths million were illiterate and thus did not vote. Others were in prison or other institutions, residents of the District of Columbia, had religious scruples against voting, or were in the

Armed Forces (and had not applied for absentee ballots).

This leaves about 15,000,000 people on whom the expenditure of $100,000,000 was wasted.

When the Constitution was written, there was no thought of spending a penny to persuade the people to vote for President, or any reason to. The electors were going to elect the President, and in only five states were the people allowed to vote for the electors. No one was interested in persuading the people to vote and a lot of people thought they shouldn't.

Gradually each state adopted the plan of having the electors chosen by popular vote, and as this happened the electors became the instruments of the voters who chose them.

Early in our country only freemen had the vote, but eventually it was extended to almost every white male adult. As the western states opened up, one of the ways in which they interested settlers was the promise of the right to vote. However, between 1778 and 1856 the original thirteen colonies established this right, and by the middle of the nineteenth century it was widespread.

Today there are five general requirements for voting:

1. Citizenship. Native-born or naturalized.
2. Residence. This may vary from six months to

two years, depending upon locality. It is intended as a proof of the good faith of residents and to prevent double voting. Without this provision, 10,000 people from Georgia could go to New Hampshire and elect a governor of their choice.

3. Legal age. Most states set the legal voting age at twenty-one, but some have lowered it on the assumption that anyone old enough to fight for his country in the armed services is old enough to vote. Georgia, Kentucky, Alaska, and Hawaii have established voting ages from eighteen to twenty.

4. Literacy. In a third of the states, voters must prove that they can read and write.

5. Registration. Those desiring to become voters are required to appear before election (or town) officials, show that they meet legal requirements, and have their names placed on the voting list. In some states these lists are permanent; in others, voters are required to re-register at intervals.

Various other states have special requirements, such as a poll tax, the refusal of the vote to mental incompetents and certain criminals.

In 1868 the Fourteenth Amendment, in one section, provided that any state which denied the right to vote to male citizens of twenty-one and over would have its representation in Congress reduced in proportion to the number of such citizens in relation to the total of all males over twenty-one years of age. This provision has never been enforced.

The Fifteenth Amendment, ratified in 1870, provides that no citizen shall be denied the vote by any state on account of race, color, or previous condition of servitude. In February 1963 President John F. Kennedy urged that this amendment be strengthened by more federal support, and that the Negroes of our population be allowed to vote.

This question, which plagues us today and harms us in the eyes of the world, is actually a very old one. Our Declaration of Independence said that "all men are created equal," but there were doubts in the minds of many Americans at that time. Like George Orwell in *Animal Farm*, some Americans still believe that "all animals are equal, but some animals are more equal than others." The struggle for true representation of all our people has been a long one, and the vote for the Negro is one of a series of battles fought in the interest of democracy.

It is interesting to note that many of the southern states, where various devices are used to prevent Negroes from voting, rank lowest in percentage of voters represented in elections and thus lack a great deal of the influence they might have.

It was not until 1920 that the right to vote was extended to women, with the adoption of the Nineteenth Amendment. The battle for this vote was a long and heated one, and many feel that its achievement may some day lead to a woman becoming President.

There are more than 100,000 polling places in America where citizens may cast their votes. Each county and city is divided into precincts, each of which contains several hundred voters. The polling place in each precinct is almost always a public building, such as a school, a police station, or a church, though some states with warm climates use tents.

Once the voter enters his polling place, the campaign is over. No political propaganda or influence is allowed, by law, in or very near a polling place.

The officials at the polling place consist of regular election officers, who check the voter against the voting list, hand out ballots, and receive them when they are completed. There are inspectors or judges of elections and watchers (representing different parties and candidates), all of whom are present to see that the rights of the voter are safeguarded.

Many years ago several states had oral voting. The voter approached the election officials, was recognized, and announced the names of his candidates aloud. There were certain defects in this system, as can be imagined, the greatest of them being that voters might be too worried about public opinion to vote as they wished.

A hundred years or so ago, a party ballot was used.

Each party printed its own, listing only its own candidates. These were given out in advance of the election and were cast in the open. Anyone who wished to divide his vote between two parties could mark out the name of the candidate he did not want and write in another, but it would be observed by everyone. Political bosses could easily control an election where party ballots were used, because it was plain to see how each person voted.

In 1888 a type of ballot called the "Australian ballot" was used in this country and still is, with various changes. The Australian ballot is printed at public expense, carries the names of all candidates, is distributed only at the polling place, and is marked in secret.

In twenty-one states the ballot lists all of the candidates for each office in a separate group, with the party of each candidate after his name. In some of these states, voting a "straight" ticket is also provided for, but in some each candidate must be voted for separately.

In some states the several parties each have a separate column of candidates. If a check mark is put in a large circle at the top of any column, it indicates a "straight" party vote, but it is almost as easy for the voter to split his vote between different parties if he wishes.

The voter who has been identified as a legally

registered voter of his precinct is given a ballot and goes into the polling place to cast his vote. If some disability hampers him, he may have the assistance of an election official in marking his ballot. When the marking is complete, he folds his ballot as directed, so that it cannot be identified, and gives it to the proper official who deposits it in the box.

Some states now have voting machines, which allow the voter to register his preference by pulling down levers. Voting machines eliminate many of the problems of voting, because they are easy to manipulate, keep the vote entirely secret, and register the total number of votes cast as the election proceeds. Their disadvantages are their cost and the fact that they occasionally break down, thus making invalid all of the votes cast in the particular broken machine.

As soon as the polls have closed (and the law says that they must be open long enough to allow every registered voter a reasonable opportunity to vote), the counting of votes begins.

America now gets the results of the election more quickly than ever before over radio and television. In some polls, special counting boards handle the tallying of votes, beginning a few hours after the polls open. In others, the count is not begun until after the final vote is cast. Where machines are used, of course, the total of votes is available as the voting progresses.

Almost all states provide for absentee voting by

those who are unable to be at the polls because of travel, illness, or service in the Armed Forces. Unfortunately, not a very large percentage of those entitled to an absentee vote make use of it.

Recent provisions for voting by those in the armed services are a big improvement over anything before, and the difference is shown in the number of votes cast. In 1942 servicemen had to write to the state Secretaries of State to send them a "war ballot." Only 28,051 members of the Armed Forces actually voted. When states enacted laws that made it easier for servicemen to vote, a total of nearly 2,800,000 took advantage of them.

In federal elections, what is known as the "short" ballot is used. Each voter is asked to help choose not more than four or five officers—the President, the Vice-President, a senator, a representative from the voter's district, and sometimes a representative from the state at large.

In state and local elections, a "long ballot" is used and the voter is asked to select people to fill a large number of offices.

There is a movement to replace all "long ballots" with short ones, in order to improve our voting. A voter in Los Angeles, for example, may be asked to vote for candidates for forty-five offices and for or against fifty-eight measures in a general election, and in Colorado the voter may have to help choose thirty officers and vote on sixteen measures.

The general democratic theory is that officers who make public policy should be elected by the people, while those who carry out policy may be appointed. It is sometimes difficult to draw the line between the two types of duties, but there is a certain tendency to allow administrators to appoint their own assistants, in order to remove such a large burden of choice from the voter.

With the best will in the world, it would be very difficult for the average voter to know enough about candidates for thirty different offices to make the wise choice in every case. When the short ballot is used, he needs less prior knowledge and should be able to vote more intelligently.

The danger in the trend toward the short ballot would be that elected officers might put too many of their friends and supporters in office, without regard for the public welfare. At any rate, this is one of the problems of our elections that needs to be solved in a way that will strengthen and uphold our democracy.

Chapter 14

THE NEW PRESIDENT

It should be easy for everyone to be an expert on presidential elections.

There is hardly an issue of a newspaper or magazine printed that does not have some information or opinions about politics, and all radio and television stations devote a certain amount of their air time to this subject. In the year of a presidential election, this coverage will be doubled and redoubled.

We can follow the fortunes of our favorite candidate, and his opponent, from long before their party nominations to the eve of election. We are told, in detail, how the campaigns are going, what issues are most important, why the voting will be light or heavy, and how the electoral votes from each state will probably go.

Just before Election Day we are provided with

score cards and information sheets by newspapers and magazines, and sometimes by companies that publish them as advertising.

We are given so much information that it is hard to see why everyone doesn't know, well in advance, just which candidate for President will be elected.

The reason we don't is that the people of America do the electing, and no one can be absolutely sure, in advance, exactly what they will do.

In the days before the election, political experts will publish their predictions and their reasons for thinking they are right. They will also provide charts for voters to follow while watching the election returns on television. These charts explain how the votes will come in from different sections of the country, and what they will mean.

The state of New York, for instance, had forty-five electoral votes in the 1960 election. The city of New York supplied about half the voters in the state, and is traditionally Democratic. The other half of the voters, in the smaller cities and rural areas, are traditionally Republican.

Both candidates, Richard Nixon and John Kennedy, wanted New York, and both of them worked hard to get it. Just before the election, experts felt that if Kennedy got more than 750,000 votes in the city of New York, he would carry the state.

The total electoral vote of 1960 was 537 votes, and

the winning candidate had to receive 269 of them. The forty-five votes of New York would help a great deal.

Each state is analyzed in this way by men who have been studying it closely for months. The history of each state is studied to see how it has voted in the past and why it has voted that way. (Some states go Republican if a majority of the voters go to the polls; others go Democratic.) In election years, states are apt to follow their historical pattern of voting—if the state is mostly Republican, it will vote that way in the presidential election because more voters go to the polls in presidential years. In "off year" elections, when the presidency is not at stake, such a state may go Democratic because so many people do not bother to vote.

In the presidential election of 1952, and in all since then, the major broadcasting systems have used electronic computers, or "brains" to tell in advance how the election was going. Before the election, information about past elections, and factors and trends in these elections, is fed into the machines. (For a specific state, this information might show that the state was balanced between the Democratic and Republican parties, but that a record turnout usually meant a Republican victory. It might also show that the previous Democratic candidate won fifty-eight per cent of the vote in city areas, and the previous Republican candidate won sixty-five per cent of the rural areas, and that more Democrats than Republicans would go to the polls when the rights of labor were a key issue.)

As the first scattered returns begin to come in from all over the country, these returns are fed into the machine to determine what they mean. Perhaps the Republican candidate shows more votes in the urban areas than his opponent—this may mean that the voting pattern has shifted, and if he can take the cities he is sure to have the rural areas as well.

In 1952, the Columbia Broadcasting System used a Univac machine and two hours after the polls closed it predicted a landslide vote for Dwight Eisenhower. The experts did not believe it, but final counts showed that the machine had given the correct electoral vote within four. In 1956, with only 300,-000 votes in, it predicted another Eisenhower victory, only thirteen votes off from the final tally given by the Electoral College.

Each year more and more faith is placed in these electronic "brains," but this does not mean that our elections are a foregone conclusion yet.

In the 1960 election, Kennedy received 300 electoral votes and Nixon 223. Fourteen electoral votes, from Mississippi and Alabama, were unpledged.

Charges of fraud were raised about the elections in Cook County, mainly in Chicago. Kennedy carried Illinois by a margin of 9,801 out of a total vote of 4,745,475. (The Socialist-Labor candidate received 10,560 votes, more than Kennedy's lead over Nixon.) If the charges of fraud were upheld, and Kennedy lost Illinois with its twenty-seven electoral votes, the fourteen unpledged votes from the South could have turned the tide against him in the Electoral College.

The vote of Illinois was not changed, and the Electoral College gave Kennedy 303 votes, Nixon 219. Out of a national popular vote of 68,335,587, Kennedy received 34,226,925 and Nixon 34,108,662.

Twice in our history the Electoral College has failed to elect a President. When this happens, the Constitution says that the House of Representatives must choose a President from the three highest on the electoral list.

In 1801 both Thomas Jefferson and Aaron Burr received seventy-three electoral votes. When the House of Representatives met to decide the winner, the Federalist party (which had lost the election) tried to secure the loyalty of Burr, whom they then offered to make President. Burr turned them down, and so Jefferson received the election.

In 1824 the electoral vote was ninety-nine for Andrew Jackson, eighty-four for John Quincy

Adams, forty-one for William H. Crawford, and thirty-seven for Henry Clay. No candidate had received a majority of all the electoral votes, and so the matter was turned over to the House of Representatives. Clay, who had the least number of votes, still had enough to command the election. The candidate who received his support would be President, and he gave it to Adams.

One of the most exciting presidential elections in our history was the contest between Samuel J. Tilden, Democrat, and Rutherford B. Hayes, Republican. By midnight on Election Day, November 7, 1876, the election had been conceded to Tilden. He had a majority of 250,000 votes over his Republican rival and had carried the doubtful states of New York, New Jersey, and Indiana.

Four newspapermen at the *New York Times* began an investigation and discovered that there was a dispute about the returns of South Carolina, Louisiana, and Florida, and a technical question about one elector in Oregon. If these twenty electoral votes were counted for Hayes, he would have 185 votes.

"Visiting statesmen" (both Republican and Democratic leaders) visited the capitals of the states and found evidence of fraud and intimidation. It seemed that Hayes had a majority in South Carolina and Tilden in Louisiana, and the vote in Florida was extremely close. The contest was taken to the courts, and two sets of returns went to the Electoral College.

A special electoral commission, of seven Democrats and seven Republicans, was appointed to rule on the legality of the electors. A fifteenth member of the commission, with the deciding vote, was to be Judge David Davis, who held independent views. Five days before the commission was to meet, Judge Davis retired from his office as judge and became a senator from Illinois. His place on the commission was taken by a Republican, a Justice Bradley.

The commission voted on a strict party basis, eight to seven, and Republican Hayes won the election.

It has been said that Tilden did not continue the battle because he feared it might lead to another Civil War, but agreed to let it go when the Democrats were promised that federal troops would be withdrawn from the South. Whether this is true or not, the troops were withdrawn shortly after the inauguration, and the era of carpetbagging in the South was ended.

Tilden had received 4,284,757 popular votes, and Hayes 4,033,950. In 1888, Grover Cleveland received 5,540,050 popular votes to 5,444,337 for Benjamin Harrison, but Cleveland received only 168 electoral votes to 233 for Harrison, who therefore became President.

One of our greatest presidents was elected by a minority of the voters. When Abraham Lincoln ran for office in 1860, he received 1,866,352 popular votes and Stephen A. Douglas 1,375,157. The other votes were split between John C. Breckinridge and John Bell, so Lincoln had a lead over his strongest opponent, but not a majority of all the votes cast.

With these exceptions, the election returns after the voting on the first Tuesday in November after the first Monday have always told us who our new President would be.

On the first Monday after the second Wednesday in December, the electors meet at their various state capitals and cast their votes for President and Vice-President. On January 6 of the following year, the votes are formally counted at a joint session of the two houses of Congress, and the president of the Senate announces the "state of the vote," just as it was done the first time for George Washington.

The result is rarely a surprise to anyone. The people of America knew, after the national party conventions, which candidate they favored. (But, so far, no one has found a sure way of discovering this information and knowing in advance how many of the people who favor each candidate will go to the polls.) The candidates know, as soon as all of the election returns are in, which one was elected.

It is a great and honorable tradition in our country that the losing candidate always accepts the election of his opponent and pledges his support to him for the welfare of our country. American voters follow his lead, and the fuss and fanfare and fighting of campaigns are buried by an overwhelming love of country until it is time for another election to begin.

Chapter 15

THE OFFICE OF PRESIDENT

The man on the balcony of Federal Hall in New York in April 1789 was dressed in dark brown, with metal buttons with an eagle on them, white stockings, a bag, and a sword.

He raised his hand and repeated the oath of office.

"I do solemnly swear that I will faithfully execute the office of President of the United States and will, to the best of my ability, preserve, protect, and defend the Constitution of the United States."

After that, although the Constitution does not require it, he gave his inaugural address. He said later that he had been more agitated and embarrassed than ever he was by the leveled cannon or pointed musket, but others said that it was a very touching occasion— marred only by President Washington's badly fitting false teeth, which made some of his words difficult to understand.

Our first President was inaugurated in April, and those after that, until recent years, in March. This meant that the former President and the other officers of our government who had been defeated in the current election were still in office until the new President took over. The reason the inauguration took place in March, although the Electoral College met in December, was the state of the roads in winter. By 1937 the Twentieth Amendment to the Constitution had changed this, and Franklin Roosevelt was the first President to be inaugurated in January.

The inaugural address has two purposes; it serves to bind up wounds received in the campaign which preceded it, and it gives the President an opportunity to explain what he intends to do while in office.

Calvin Coolidge was the first President whose inaugural address was delivered over the radio to millions of Americans, and now we take for granted that we shall be able to see as well as hear the inaugural, though we may be thousands of miles from Washington when it takes place.

The inauguration of a President may reflect a great deal of his personality and his attitude toward his new position. When Andrew Jackson was elected, the working people and farmers of America felt that the old line of "aristocratic" Presidents had been broken.

A commentator said, "It was a proud day for the people. General Jackson is *their own* President."

Daniel Webster wrote to a friend, "Nobody knows what he will do when he arrives . . . my opinion is that when he comes he will bring a breeze with him . . . which way it will blow, I cannot tell . . . My *fear* is much stronger than my *hope*."

Jackson's friends followed him into Washington and swarmed through the city. Someone wrote, "It was like the inundation of northern barbarians into Rome. Strange faces filled every public place and every face seemed to bear defiance on its brow."

The reception following the inauguration created a public scandal to those who believed in dignity in government. A motley crowd entered the White House, stood on damask-covered chairs in muddy boots, overturned pails of orange punch, broke glasses, and pushed each other around in their eagerness to see the President and shake his hand.

After the inauguration, the President settles down to his duties, and the country settles down to watch him—and, being America, to decide to replace him if it seems best for the country.

Most of us respect and support our President, no matter how we felt about him during the campaign, and he can be sure of this loyalty and trust. He can be equally sure that those who work for him while he is in office will work just as diligently against him in the next campaign if they feel another man could do the job better.

We think of presidential campaigns as lasting from before the primaries and/or the great party conventions until the polls close on the first Tuesday after the first Monday in November, but they are really going on all the time.

Immediately after the election several defeated candidates have begun work on their next campaign, and presidential hopefuls are always seeking the public eye so their chances will be better in a future election.

More than this, the off-year elections will come up in two years. Those who do not approve of the President by that time may work hard to elect senators and congressmen of the opposite party in order to combat him on legislation.

In another phase of our political activities, reformers are always at work trying to change the way in which we elect our President.

Is the Electoral College a fair and just representation of the will of the people? Some of our Presidents have had a larger popular vote than the winner, but have not won the most electoral votes. Is this right?

Because the Electoral College has become the rubber stamp of the voters, some think it should be abolished completely. This might amount to nothing more than getting rid of the formality of the Electoral

College, which is now little more than a ceremony.

In one version of this plan, it has been suggested that each state should return the same electoral votes in relation to its population that it has now, but these votes should go immediately to the President rather than to the electors.

It has been proposed that the popular votes of the country should elect the President, which would have meant that some of the Presidents we have had would not have won the election. The opponents of this plan point out that it would increase the influence of the heavily populated states and decrease the influence of the sparsely populated ones. (This was a problem our founding fathers had to face when they drew up the Constitution. The smaller states did not want to be run by the larger ones, and so our system of representation was set up.)

If such a system should be adopted, it would reduce the power of the South considerably. The total vote of the South is very small compared to its actual population, since so large a number of its people are Negroes who are prevented in different ways from voting.

In 1950 a plan called the Lodge-Gossett resolution was placed before the nation as a proposed constitutional Amendment.

This plan would allow each state the same number of electors as the present system; each candidate for

President would be given electoral votes and fractions thereof in each state in proportion to his popular vote in the state; a candidate who received a majority or plurality of the electoral votes, providing the plurality was forty per cent of the total, would be elected President, and if no candidate received a plurality of forty per cent, then the two houses of Congress in joint session, the members voting individually, would choose the President from the two candidates having the highest number of electoral votes.

The difference in this plan is that each state could split its electoral votes. As it is now, if the Republican electors receive the majority of the votes, they carry all the electoral votes of the state. Under the Lodge plan, the electoral votes in each state would be divided according to the percentage of the popular votes. Thus if the Republicans carried two thirds of the popular vote in New York, they would receive only two thirds of the electoral votes, instead of all of them. The other third would go to the other party, or parties, according to their percentage of the popular vote.

With the Lodge plan, we would have had some different Presidents: Tilden instead of Hayes, Hancock instead of Garfield, Cleveland instead of Harrison, and Bryan instead of McKinley.

Opponents of this plan point out, since the vote of

the South is based on a very restricted suffrage, the Democratic vote for the entire country would be very high in electoral elections and low in popular vote while the Republican vote would be just the opposite.

Several years ago the presidential primary was instituted as a method of giving the voters a better chance of selecting candidates for President, but this has not worked well. Laws governing primaries are different in different states, so that in some the people vote for their delegates to national conventions without requiring these delegates to vote for specific candidates; in others, few of the presidential candidates enter, so the voter does not have a choice among all of the men who will run for office.

The presidential primary convention problem is like the old question of which came first, the chicken or the egg. When the convention meets, all likely candidates are put on view, and the party platform is assembled; if the voters at the primaries had this information in advance, they could make a reasonable choice. The voters at the primary can hardly create a platform by voting, nor can they vote for all potential candidates if their names are not before them.

Perhaps, as with the Electoral College plan, reforms wil come about that will make our system of selecting and electing a President much better than it is. If this happens, it will be done by the citizens of our country who are now growing up.

There are those who feel that our political party system has defects, and that the strength of the two major parties is too great. While there may be abuses of power within each of the parties, there are certain things that we must remember.

When the right to vote became more widespread, the actual number of voters did not grow as rapidly as had been expected. As the two major political parties began to grow and gain more members, the number of those who voted increased rapidly.

People who care very much about one party or the other are more apt to vote than those who do not. The whole history of our country has shown an increasing effort to get more people to the polls in order to increase our democracy. We must remember that the basic principle upon which democracy is founded is that governments should exist by the consent of the governed. Those who do not vote are not helping to shape the government which governs them.

As Thomas Jefferson said in 1821, "I know of no safe depository of the ultimate powers of society but the people themselves; and if we think them not enlightened enough to exercise their control with a wholesome discretion, the remedy is not to take it from them, but to inform their discretion by education."

If we object to political parties or conventions or any of the other forces which play so large a role in selecting our President, we should ask ourselves how much power they have and how they got that power.

In the long run our Presidents are elected, and our country governed, by the people who care. In our right to vote we have been given the instrument by which we can express our own concern about our government, and the more of us who use this instrument, the more our government will reflect our needs, wishes, and ideas.

When our original thirteen colonies began, only a limited number of white adult male citizens were allowed to vote. Before the Revolution against England, the whole population was not persuaded that it was a good idea to revolt. A very few people who cared very much, who believed that the English government was doing what no government had the right to do, stirred up the others. They made speeches, wrote articles, and talked to everyone they saw about how a government should be run, until the idea of freedom blazed into a flame that swept through the new country.

After the Revolution, each state was governed by a separate government, some modeled very closely after the same constitutions that had been in effect during the rule of England. Debtors' prisons existed; not more than one fourth of all white male citizens were allowed to vote.

A few courageous men saw the need for a strong central government and began the same sort of campaign that had brought about the Revolution to bring it into being.

When the Constitution was written, its framers may have had a very low opinion of the intelligence and ability of the average man and even of the possible one fourth of our adult male population which could vote. However, they realized that no government would be adopted which the people could not be persuaded to accept.

In America, even those without the vote had learned to be effective in forming public opinion. They could join in discussion, express their opinions, write letters, and make as much fuss as possible until they persuaded others to join them.

All of this had to be taken into consideration when the Constitution was written. It is less elaborate than many of the state constitutions, and one reason is surely the attempt to leave out everything that would lose votes.

Even so, the Constitution would not have been adopted if those who believed in it had not put up a terrific battle to gain support for it—and then only when the people had been assured that the rights mentioned in the Declaration of Independence, and for which they had fought, would be included in the amendments called our Bill of Rights.

The new American government was weak and uncertain, a pygmy in a world of giants. She was made strong and flourishing by all of the people who worked and suffered and spoke their minds about both her faults and virtues.

Very few things in our democratic way of life are as important to us as our right to elect a President, but this right was not given to us, as we now enjoy it, by our founding fathers. It came about as the attitude of our country changed, and the electors were turned into people who followed the will of the voters, rather than people superior to the voters who selected the best man for President.

Everything that we have and every tradition that gives us freedom began in the mind of one man as an idea which he persuaded others to support. Although we say that the majority rules, most of the principles of our government began through the efforts of a small but impassioned group who eventually grew into a majority.

Each voter is a minority. He has only one vote, one voice, one tiny sphere of influence, and yet he can become as powerful as he wishes. He can work to improve our government in the way he chooses, by helping the party of his choice, by starting another party, by running for office or helping to elect someone else, by writing letters to newspapers and to his congressman, by trying to change laws he feels are unfair.

On the other hand, he can make himself count for nothing as a citizen of America. He can stay away from the polls, he can refrain from expressing an opinion, he can believe that the whole country is run by bosses who pay no attention to him, and he can refuse to care what happens in elections.

America is not perfect. It contains too many people, with too many different opinions, to be that. Not one of our elected officials, not even our President, is perfect. Neither our forefathers nor our political authorities today have thought that the voters of America were so wise and all-intelligent that they could do no wrong. Our system of voting is designed for imperfect people, providing a way in which the right will have the best possible chance to triumph.

More than anything else, our country is a huge, confusing, conflicting turmoil of activity in which things change constantly and people think differently all of the time. Our government allows us to make mistakes without endangering our welfare permanently, because it gives us the method to correct them.

We are, in the long run, and by our own efforts or lack of them, governed as well as we deserve to be. Because of the vast powers put in our hands by our form of elections, we can blame no one but ourselves if our country is not run the way we like.

Each time we go to the polls to mark our ballots, we should echo the words Carl Schurz said to the United States Senate in 1872:

"Our country, right or wrong! When right, to keep it right; when wrong, to be put right!"

INDEX

Electors, cast votes, 137; in Constitution, 51, 52, 53; presidential, 3
Electoral college, 134, 142, 143, 145; votes, 131, 132

Farley, James, 84
Favorite sons, 89
Four Freedoms, 7, 8
Freemen, 7, 8, 122
Fremont, John C., 118

Gavel, 26, 27
Grant, Ulysses S., 65

Hamilton, Alexander, 53
Hancock, General Winfield Scott, 101
Harding, Warren G., 89, 90
Harrison, Benjamin, 136
Harrison, William Henry, 67, 68, 97, 103
Hayes, Rutherford B., 135, 136
Hendricks, Thomas, 101
Henry, Patrick, 49, 57
Hoover, Herbert, 102
Humphrey, Hubert, 86

Inauguration, 140, 141; first, 139, 140
Ingersoll, Robert G., 102

Jackson, Andrew, 67, 134, 140, 141
Jefferson, Thomas, 66, 107, 134, 146
Judd, Norman B., 99

Kefauver, Estes, 73, 99, 100
Kennedy, John F., 66, 73, 94, 124, 131, 133, 134

Lincoln, Abraham, 95, 98, 99, 137

Lodge-Gossett Resolution, 142, 143

Marcy, William L., 101
Massachusetts Bay Colony, 17
McClellan, George, 87
Mudslinging, 118, 119

Nixon, Richard, 131, 133, 134
National Party Conventions, 75, 76, 77, 78; accrediting delegates, 80, 81; balloting, 103, 104, 105; Committee on Permanent Organization, 84; Committee on Credentials, 81; delegates to, 76, 77, 78; demonstrations, 99, 104, 105, 107; first, 72; keynote speech, 82, 83; nominating speeches, 98, 102; platform, 85, 86, 87, 88; roll call, 98, 100; Rules Committee, 84; size of, 80; unit rule, 100

Pierce, Franklin, 101, 118
Political party, membership in, 110
Political parties, early American, 62, 63; Republican and Democratic, 63, 64, 65
Poll tax, 123
Polling places, 125
Precincts, 125
President, assumed requirements of, 66; eligibility for, 50, 51; first elected, 3; how selected, 6–7; power of, 4, 5; requirements for, 69, 93, 94, 95, 96, 97; title chosen, 46, 47

153

Biography of Duane Bradley

Duane Bradley has been interested in the workings of democracy since childhood. She recalls a book which she read then which "explained so clearly and dramatically how Communism works that I have wished for years to write a book which would make the American idea as clear to our young people." ELECTING A PRESIDENT is the result of that long-held wish, and is based on the premise that "the most important individual in a presidential election is not the one who is elected, but the individual voter."

Duane Bradley (Mrs. George Sanborn in private life) was born in Iowa and spent her childhood in the rich farming areas of that state and Missouri, eventually moving to southern California where she worked on newspapers for a number of years.

During World War II she and her family saw more of these United States as her husband's army service assignments took them to Washington, Rhode Island, and Delaware. By the end of the war they had settled in the small New Hampshire town where they now live and from which her husband's family originally came. Her early interest in writing expressed itself in short verses and stories and by her teens she had won a prize in a national short story contest. She has published six other books for children and young people—and is always working on her latest enthusiasm. Right now it is the nature and workings of democracy.